Elephant Wings to Freedom

MOTHER NATURE'S DREAM

Chaitanya Sridhar

Chennai • Bangalore

CLEVER FOX PUBLISHING
Chennai, India

Published by CLEVER FOX PUBLISHING 2025
Copyright © Dr. Chaitanya Sridhar 2025
Editor - Sonam Kala

All Rights Reserved.
Paperback ISBN: 978-93-67075-97-5
Hardback ISBN: 978-93-67070-26-0

This book has been published with all reasonable efforts taken to make the material error-free after the consent of the author. No part of this book shall be used, reproduced in any manner whatsoever without written permission from the author, except in the case of brief quotations embodied in critical articles and reviews.

The Author of this book is solely responsible and liable for its content including but not limited to the views, representations, descriptions, statements, information, opinions and references ["Content"]. The Content of this book shall not constitute or be construed or deemed to reflect the opinion or expression of the Publisher or Editor. Neither the Publisher nor Editor endorse or approve the Content of this book or guarantee the reliability, accuracy or completeness of the Content published herein and do not make any representations or warranties of any kind, express or implied, including but not limited to the implied warranties of merchantability, fitness for a particular purpose. The Publisher and Editor shall not be liable whatsoever for any errors, omissions, whether such errors or omissions result from negligence, accident, or any other cause or claims for loss or damages of any kind, including without limitation, indirect or consequential loss or damage arising out of use, inability to use, or about the reliability, accuracy or sufficiency of the information contained in this book.

TESTIMONIALS

"*Elephant Wings to Freedom* is masterfully a beautifully woven tapestry of personal connection, cultural reverence, and profound ecological wisdom. The author's remarkable journey, from childhood wonder to profound understanding, resonates powerfully with the timeless bond between elephants and humanity. With lyrical storytelling and deep insight, this remarkable book is undoubtedly an inspiring and essential read for anyone who fondly cherishes wildlife, spirituality, and the profound lessons elephants offer us. A heartfelt tribute to the gentle giants who share our world."

– **Byju. H, Author, Matriarch**

"I am so excited about this book! I could imagine this scene and feel everything from walking on the grass bare feet to imagining looking into an animal's eye, so beautifully written."

– **Maana Patel, Olympian**

"Gripping and effortless narrative with vivid imagery. The connection to nature and well-being is impactful. Thoughtfully balanced exercises make the journey personal and deeply engaging."

– **Manasa K.S. Jungian Psychoanalyst & Founder, BSAP**

"The chapters exude with bewilderment of the gentle giants. Communication and a connect between the elephants and the author is palpable."

– **Prabha Dev, Heritage Beku**

"Meeting (Elephant) Leela, for the first time you shared a certain innocence, you came to meet her without an agenda or 'know-how'— and you waited for her to choose, to initiate the contact and how it would unfold. You responded intuitively, like the mother with her baby, attuned to her queues, vocals and actions. A world of connection and deep healing happened between you."

– Marian Dunlea, author and creator of BodyDreaming

Elephant Wings to Freedom

MOTHER NATURE'S DREAM

DR. CHAITANYA SRIDHAR

Photograph Credits

Main Cover Photograph by Pravin Shanmughanandam

Back Cover Photograph by Sujata Khanna

"An elephant herd enjoying a very comfortable, intimate moment, as they nap at the edge of a Shola forest patch, with a very young calf amongst them.

There are very few spaces in the wild for the largest mammals on land, to be themselves, and thrive with absolute freedom and guaranteed safety. When Mother Nature is undisturbed and not meddled with, she can hold everyone safe in her protective arms."

– Pravin Shanmughanandam

Back Cover

"The all-knowing eyes and inspiration for the book."

Dedication

To the gentle giants and those serving the elephants.

"A creature with the breath of life.

Anima- a breeze, then breath, then soul

Anima."

– Heathcote Williams

DISCLAIMER

The inspiration for this book comes from my profound bond with elephants and my quest to improve their situation. It is a personal account of my experiences and understanding of elephants and their world, shaped through direct interactions with these magnificent beings and those dedicated to their well-being. This work is a culmination of years of engagement with elephant conservationists and welfare advocates passionately involved in this space.

Beyond just conservation, this book delves into depth psychology—a subject close to me as a sport and depth psychologist. However, it extends far beyond the academic realm, offering a perspective that emerges from a sacred space of reverence and personal transformation.

I encourage readers to embrace what resonates with them and leave behind what does not. As an Indian, I hold deep respect for all philosophies and perspectives, and no offence is intended in any way. These are my personal reflections, and this book approaches elephants through a spiritual and psychological lens, inviting you to explore and connect in your own way.

Knowing these gentle giants has transformed me in profound ways, and I hope these writings inspire and guide you toward goodness.

ELEPHANT WINGS TO FREEDOM

To hold the trunk of an elephant and listen to its rumbles is akin to being embraced by the Great Cosmic Mother herself.

Serving these gentle giants has truly been the privilege of a lifetime.

May the elephants touch your heart and awaken the depths of your soul—so that you, too, are inspired to join the movement to protect our heritage species, before it's too late.

– Dr. Chaitanya Sridhar

CONTENTS

Testimonials .... *iii*
Disclaimer .... *viii*
Foreword .... *xiii*
Editor's Note .... *xv*
Preface .... *xvi*
Introduction .... *xix*

Section 1: Culture And Mystery 1
Chapter 1. Airavata ~ An Inner Calling 2
Chapter 2. Ganesha ~ The Alchemical God 20
Chapter 3. Palakapya: The First Conservationist ~ Legacy for Current State of Elephants 38

Section 2: Psyche, Soul, And Symbolism 55
Chapter 4. Dream Significance and Befriending the Other 56
Chapter 5. My Little One ~ Leela and Our Journey 72
Chapter 6. Elephant Totem ~ Symbol of the Higher Self 90

Section 3: Sacred Ecology 107
Chapter 7. Reconnecting to Nature and Gaia 108
Chapter 8. Sacred Elephants 124
Chapter 9. Anima Mundi ~ The World Soul Beckons 142

Epilogue *160*
Acknowledgments *164*
Reference & Bibliography *166*
Appendix *169*
About AANE *170*
A Note from the Author *171*

FOREWORD

*I*t is with great honour that I write this foreword for Elephant Wings to Freedom, a book that opens a portal into the majestic world of elephants and their profound connection with humanity. This book is a tribute not only to these magnificent creatures but also to the intricate web of life they represent. It offers a deep dive into various aspects of elephants, their history of resilience, compassion and coexistence. Through its pages, users will experience an undeniable connection with the elephants.

Dr. Chaitanya has masterfully constructed together culture, psychology, and personal reflection to present a work that is both deeply insightful and emotionally stirring. She takes us beyond scientific facts into the heart of their existence and historical significance, making us question their protection as not just a conservation issue but a reflection of our collective society.

My personal experience with Dr. Chaitanya's sports psychology sessions was transformative, as she guided me in grounding myself, processing challenges, and finding inner strength.

Being an animal lover myself, I resonated deeply with Dr. Chaitanya's discussions on elephants and the valuable lessons they can teach us in our own journeys as athletes. She has helped me stay in sync with nature, teaching me how to find strength and stillness, qualities essential for me as an athlete, all while drawing lessons from the natural world. Through her guidance, I have come to understand the importance of connecting with nature and recognising that I am a part of it.

This approach has fostered my holistic development, allowing me to transcend my role as a performance-driven athlete. Elephant Wings to Freedom is a thoughtfully crafted guide that takes readers on a transformative journey from addiction to connection, from self-centeredness to selflessness, and from giving up to giving back—all while embracing growth and coexistence with the world around us.

In our fast-paced lives today, we often overlook the small wonders around us and fail to grasp the beauty of life when we are in harmony with nature. This book goes beyond being a mere tribute to elephants; it serves as a call to action, a contemplation of our humanity, and a guide to self-discovery. It speaks with the dreamer, the conservationist, the spiritual seeker, and the lover of life within each of us.

As you flip through these pages, may you sense the wisdom of the elephants, listen to the whispers of Mother Earth, and find inspiration to walk gently yet purposefully on this planet. May this work awaken a deeper connection, compassion, and responsibility towards all living beings.

Thank you, Dr. Chaitanya, for being you. Thank you for always bringing a smile to my face during our sessions. No matter how challenging my struggles may be, I always feel a sense of relief and joy just knowing I'll be meeting with you. You have been an integral part of my journey, and your compassion and kindness mean the world to me. I really look up to you for the incredible work you do with the elephants, and I am certain it will leave a lasting impact on all who read it.

Maana Patel, Olympian
Indian Backstroke Swimmer & an Avid Animal Lover

EDITOR'S NOTE

'Elephant Wings to Freedom' is emerging at a time when there is a pressing need for paradigm shifts in the natural world and the way humans have been living. Our resources are depleting as are the populations of elephants and forests. The significance of such a book that bridges science, culture and wildlife cannot be overstated. As the editor, it has been both an honour and a challenging undertaking that the book retains its profound depths, raw authenticity and emotional core, exactly as the author envisioned.

Dr. Chaitanya's unique blend of backgrounds bring a fresh multidimensional approach to understanding elephants, viewing them not only as biological beings but as symbolic and sentient creatures. Throughout the project and editorial process, I aimed to preserve the sincerity of her voice while ensuring that the message remains clear, impactful and immersive for the diverse readership.

This book is for those who seek to understand elephants beyond their physical demeanour—the conservationist seeking urgency, the psychologist searching for symbolic meaning, the nature enthusiast drawn to the wisdom of the wild and others who believe that books have the power to inspire positive change. Its structure seamlessly integrates across each section, allowing every reader something to resonate with.

Being part of this mystical journey into the elephant world and witnessing the creation of this one-of-a-kind book has been a privilege and humbling experience. I hope that readers not only develop a strong sense of responsibility for elephants but also gain a deeper understanding of themselves and develop a heightened awareness of their place within the interconnected web of life on Earth. I am certain this book will spark crucial dialogues, motivate action and reignite a sense of awe for elephants.

Sonam Kala
Project Consultant, AANE Core Member & Elephantophile

PREFACE

What is it about elephants that fascinate us?

This is a question I often reflect upon, especially when I think back to my childhood. As a young child, I would hear the enchanting songs of *Anne Bantu Aane* in Kannada. The lyrics, which translate to 'here comes the elephant,' filled me with a sense of awe and wonder. The song would then go on to describe the elephant's appearance, behaviour, and unique personality. In retrospect, I ponder if it was in those moments that my fascination with elephants, or 'Elez,' as I lovingly call them, first sparked. During my niece's early years, I would often sing the same song to her. It was at this time that elephants began to have a presence in my life.

The journey has been truly remarkable. I never could have imagined that our lives would become so intertwined, and that I would be entrusted with the responsibility and privilege of connecting with them first and then sharing about their magnificence and connection to our ancient bond through this book, and to the depths of wisdom that they hold to the world.

Along the way, I have been touched and supported by many incredible individuals: elephant researchers, welfare advocates, conservationists, animal communicators, and, most importantly, the elephants themselves. These gentle giants first started appearing in my dreams and I felt in awe from the moment I woke up. I gradually came to realise, through recurring dreams, that there was an uncharted realm worth exploring. The journey started with a powerful surge of energy, setting the tone for what was to come.

Since developing a deep fascination with the symbolic significance of elephants, my passion for them has only grown. In fact, my dedication to these majestic creatures led me to give a talk about the symbolism of elephants in late 2020. At this time, we also established our group, AANE (All About Nature of Elephants). Our primary goal was to convey a distinctive message to a broader audience. As I have ventured into the realm of elephant welfare and conservation, the impact on

Preface

both myself and the group has been profound. Our initial purpose transformed into a movement dedicated to preserving this magnificent species.

I set the book aside for a while, letting it simmer in the depths of my psyche. Now, it seems like the perfect time to bring it to life. The central question I aim to explore is: how can we restore the elephant wings?

How do we support them towards freedom?

What are we holding captive in our own self that we want to keep the elephants as captive?

A single elephant has the power to destroy an entire village, yet it refrains. It remains quiet unless provoked. It makes me question whether we are truly an evolved species or merely dominant and inflated beings. Perhaps they have come to aid us, the lesser-evolved human race. This is the sentiment that resonates deeply within me. I intend to intertwine my own experience with them, our shared journey, and the lessons we can extract from it.

For those of us seeking growth, there is an urgent need to address the existing imbalance and the underlying restlessness within our own species. What is nature trying to communicate? What messages do these beings carry? Of course, there are numerous sources through which these messages can be conveyed. For me, it is through elephants, and I am open to allowing them to guide.

Anecdotes will be shared since I have had the privilege of sharing my life with these magnificent creatures. I will bring these stories forward to further enhance the narrative. As a Sports and Depth Psychologist, I will also incorporate relevant examples to explore the connection between the two worlds. This union promises to be intriguing, just as it has been in my own life, effortlessly blending both these worlds.

During my Jungian interview in early 2020, the interviewers suggested that my deep connection might indicate that I could serve as a link between elephants and humans. As elephants became a major part of my life, I slowly started to comprehend and eventually, everything fell into alignment. With this newfound connection came the responsibility of conveying their message, and this book serves as one way to do so. I am often told that I light up when I begin to speak about them, and I hope their message lightens up your path.

Welcome to this endeavour. Welcome to the world of the 'elephantine spirit', where we can all grow in magnanimity and create space for our personal development, well-being, the growth of elephants, humanity, and Mother Earth.

INTRODUCTION

*E*lephants have walked alongside humanity for millennia—symbols of wisdom, gentleness, and spiritual power. They have been held in high regard across various cultures and traditions, regarded as sacred messengers, defenders of nature, and custodians of ancient knowledge. Unfortunately, their very existence is now endangered, reflecting the delicate state of our own connection with the natural world.

Elephant Wings to Freedom is an exploration and a journey far beyond the animal kingdom, not only to understand their role in history but to uncover the deeper truths they hold about ourselves and the world we inhabit.

Why Elephants? Why This Book?

I have always believed that stories shape the way we understand the world. This book was born from a personal connection—an unspoken dialogue with elephants that began in childhood and evolved into a lifelong exploration. This book features conversations I've had with people—conservationists among them—working for the welfare and dignified treatment of elephants in captivity and the wild. These interactions have allowed me to gain a deeper understanding of the issue at its core.

In addition, you will come across thought-provoking inquiries that prompt us to introspect if we are contributing to a society that consumes itself or if we appreciate and respect the significance of every species in our ecosystem. It is of utmost importance to recognise that Earth is a shared home, designed for the well-being of every living being, and it simply cannot thrive without the other.

What to Expect in This Book

This book is divided into three key sections, each offering a unique perspective on the role of elephants in human history, psychology, and environmental consciousness:

Culture & Mystery – Exploring the rich tapestry of legends surrounding elephants from Airavata, the celestial elephant, to the transformative wisdom of Ganesha, and the legendary conservationist Palakapya, these chapters portray elephants as more of symbols of reverence, emphasising their spiritual and cultural significance in Indian heritage.

Psyche, Soul & Symbolism – Drawing experience from Depth Psychology and connecting sports as an angle. This section explores the powerful totems via dreams and archetypes. The story of *Leela*, a cherished elephant, becomes a gateway to understanding the profound emotional intelligence of these beings.

Sacred Ecology – The elephants are considered essential architects of nature. Their presence shapes ecosystems, nurtures biodiversity, and teaches us about harmony with the planet. This section connects their existence to the broader theme of Gaia and *Anima Mundi*—the world soul—urging us to rekindle our bond with nature and our own soul.

About typography

Certain words, such as "field" and "space" are meant for psychological and metaphysical contexts. These concepts are unique perspectives, and I encourage you to take them in that stride.

An Invitation to Walk with Elephants as a Collective

At its core, Elephant Wings to Freedom is more than just a book about elephants—it is a powerful narrative of change that calls us to awaken something deep within ourselves. In their quiet presence, we find reflections of our own inner landscapes. Their stories are not just tales of the wild but profound lessons.

As you turn these pages, may you step into their world with open eyes and an open heart. May you find wisdom in their silence, strength in their resilience, and inspiration in their journey. The elephants are calling—will you contribute to setting them to fly freely?

SECTION 1
CULTURE AND MYSTERY

Chapter 1

AIRAVATA ~ AN INNER CALLING

Behold, here comes *Airavata*.
The mighty, gentle giant,
believed to be the king of Elephants.
The loyal companion and *vahana*[1] of Indra,
The prime *diggaja*[2], guarding the universe.
The harbinger of rain, bringing joy to the world.
Smiling tolerantly at the younger self-obsessed human species.
May we open our hearts and mind,
as he benevolently blesses with his trunk-full of wisdom.—CS. [3]

Airavata is in this *space*[4]. Who is *Airavata*? Before we get into the details, I would like you to find a serene space and take time to read the passage again. I invite you to focus gently to see what unfolds in your space. Imagine this divine being emerging from an egg, accompanied by the mystic syllables sung by *Brahma*[5]. How is he appearing to you in your imagination? Most importantly, how do you feel—body, mind and soul?

Now, I ask you to see him emerging from the ocean—pristine white, symbolising purity and divinity. What is happening to you? Where do you find the power? How is your body? Invite his guidance and begin to notice your dreams and synchronicities. Invoke his benevolence and guardian spirit to your life, especially if there are challenging areas—be it health, relations, or work.

This was *Airavata* himself, guiding me, and I am following the lead. Take a moment to pause and wonder how this impacted you. Are you feeling connected or resistant, or perhaps another emotion?

As a depth psychologist, I love playing with images as visuals are powerful and *Airavata* stands for magnanimity, loyalty and compassion, among other attributes. To make this more personal, let's draw on our own inner imagery.

I would be thrilled if we could establish a relationship with the elephant spirit right from the book's outset. When you begin this journey, you will be delighted to discover how their guidance assists you in various ways.

During my first visit to the Elephant field station in Bannerghatta, a region in Bengaluru, accompanied by a team member. Naturally, we were both eager to see the elephants during our stay. At night, I had a vivid dream of an elephant standing by the left side of the bed near the window. The dream seemed intensely real, and when I woke up, I experienced a sense of awe and warmth. To my surprise, the elephant tracker informed us that a small herd of elephants had actually passed through the area where we were staying. Indeed, we were dejected that we missed out on seeing them, but later I felt they were with us in the *field*[6] and in my psyche. It took me some time to fully grasp the deeper meaning behind it.

Bannerghatta holds a special place in my heart because of its vital elephant corridor, a pathway that elephants used to traverse. Being welcomed by these benevolent beings in the dreamscape seemed a beautiful gesture. It feels surreal, the interconnection between the inner and outer worlds, which happens to be one of the central themes of this book. As we progress through the upcoming chapters, we will delve into the intricacies of dreams in great detail.

Turning our attention back to Airavata, initiate by asking about your association with *Airavata*. This is more of an exploration, venturing into the very essence of this being instead of just providing a summary.

Divine Ancestry

Airavata has multiple meanings associated with his name, reflecting his lineage. According to the *Ramayana*[7], he is the son of *Iravati*[8], who is a descendant of the sage *Kashyapa*[9]. This explains one of the primary meanings of his name—*Airavata*, which signifies belonging to *Iravati*, 'the child of water.' It is worth noting that *Iravati* is also a river, emphasising *Airavata's* connection to rain and fertility. Furthermore, he is known by other names such as *abhra-matanga*—'the elephant of the clouds,' *naga-mala*—'the fighting elephant', and *arkasodara*—'the brother of the sun'. These names represent the qualities he embodies, including rain, bravery, loyalty and nobility.

As we dive into the mystery of this majestic giant, which has been in the collective psyche of humans throughout ancient and modern times, we find its presence embedded in lores, temples, movies and artefacts. Not only does it hold significance in various cultures, but it also appears on the flags of Siam (Thailand) and Laos, becoming an emblem of these countries.

Tamil Nadu is home to the impressive *Airavatesvara* temple, which is dedicated to Lord *Shiva*[10]. The temple derives its name from *Airavata*, the holy elephant that regained its original white hue after taking a bath in the temple's sacred lake.

I find it intriguing to contemplate the reasons behind our fascination with *Airavata, the divine elephant, and his earthly brethren.* It makes me wonder if they somehow tap into our ancient connection and consciousness, serving as a gentle nudge to awaken and reconnect to our true divine purpose.

Interestingly enough, there are two distinct versions of his birth and ancestry. According to the *Matangalila*, an elephant treatise, his origins can be traced back to Brahma. As per the legend, Brahma created *Airavata* by singing divine hymns, upon the egg laid by *Garuda*[11]. *Airavata*, the majestic king of elephants, is described as having four tusks and seven trunks, a truly awe-inspiring sight. As promised, he was then gifted to *Indra*, the god of rain and storms, serving as a befitting vahana (carrier) for the king of gods.

Pause and contemplate the significance of having the mighty *Airavata as a celestial mount to traverse the world.* Could this symbolism extend beyond the literal interpretation?

The Majestic Carrier

Why was *Airavata*—the elephant chosen, rather than a lion or a phoenix? We will explore deeper into this aspect, as it represents a sacred pair (alliance), perhaps as an ideal to that of an elephant and a *mahout*—an elephant keeper, where *Airavata* consistently defends and rescues his master.

I have been curious about the skilled mahouts from tribes like the *Malasars*[12] and *Jainu Kurubas*[13], who have a longstanding tradition in elephant management. The belief is that elephants do not just listen to commands but rather respond because of the connection formed. They will not communicate with just anyone—it is a relationship built on trust, patience, and love.

In the next section, we will see the bond I have built with an elephant, 'my little one—Leela' even though she is not so little, standing at nine feet tall and in the prime of her age.

One legend that I immensely enjoy is about *Airavata*, who played a crucial role in capturing water and showering rain, thus bringing blessings to the earth. As per sources, Indra was worried about water being trapped in *pataloka*[14] (underworld realm) and could not find a solution. *Airavata* uses his elongated trunk to draw water, which he pours into the clouds. Indra then strikes the clouds, causing rain to benefit our planet Earth, not only humans.

This story echoes a beautiful quote, *"an elephant's head is close to the heavens and its trunk close to the earth. It symbolises the union of these two extremes—the cosmic and the human."*—(Dr. Bedi, 2013).

Imagine the awe-inspiring image of an elephant trunk, capable of sending powerful vibrations through the very earth it stands upon, reaching up to the heavens above. Picture yourself holding onto this extraordinary vision, as it symbolises the profound connection between earthly sensations and heavenly intuition. It represents the beautiful amalgamation of sacred masculine and feminine energies of heaven and earth, intertwining in perfect harmony.

In our society, we often have a narrow viewpoint. The trunk, on the other hand, represents a symbol of union that exists both in our inner and outer worlds. What is this symbol trying to suggest? Rather than relying solely on logical thinking, allow the answer to emerge from the depths of your being. It may come in the form of a word, an image, a feeling, or a sensation. Embrace it, ponder upon it, and reflect on its meaning.

I see *Airavata* as a 'symbol of wholeness', representing the potential for us to tap into an empowered energy or state. Take a moment to explore what other thoughts or ideas arise within you, as there is truly no single definitive answer to this.

Alchemical Process

The *Vishnu Purana*[15] presents an alternate version where *Airavata's* involvement in the ocean churning is attributed to sage *Dhurvasa's*[16] curse, which was a consequence of the elephant trampling Indra's garland of flowers. It is debatable whether *Airavata* should be blamed for the disturbance caused by the bees swarming around the garland. The sage's anger stemmed from the fact that the flowers symbolise *Lakshmi*[17], and he cursed all the Gods to lose their youth as a result. The only solution to this curse was to obtain the *amrit* (elixir) through the process of ocean churning. Regardless of whether *Airavata* was truly at fault, he emerged as one of the '*Navaratnas*'—the nine jewels.

We will now delve into the symbolism of the majestic white elephant gracefully emerging from the depths of the ocean. The ocean churning can be seen as the inner journey to the depths. This is elaborated by Dr. Carl Jung, a psychiatrist, psychoanalyst and the founder of analytical psychology. His pivotal work was on unravelling the psyche through dreams and archetypes.

After churning for aeons, the Gods, with the help of the *asuras* (vices), were finally able to reach the *amrit* (elixir). Similarly, when we begin our inner/spiritual work, we need to work on our *asuras* (the vices) and strengthen our *devas* (virtues). The *Trimurtis*[18] blessed this effort, with *Krishna*[19] supporting 'Mount Mandara' as a tortoise (the *Kurma Avatar*[20]) and *Shiva* drinking the poison, earning the name *Neelakantha* (the one with the blue throat).

This signifies the guidance and shielding we need whilst journeying on the arduous inner work, so we don't lose our way. In this churning, *Airavata* emerged as a milky white elephant. What could this be signifying? The emergence of *Airavata*, one of the celestial beings, from the ocean was the culmination of tremendous work which emerged as a precious gift.

In the Jungian language, we describe the process of inner work as a '*transformation into gold*'. This metaphor symbolises the concept that by consistently focusing on the inner work, similar to the churning of the ocean in *Samudra Manthan*[21], profound transformations can take place.

This is when *Airavata* manifests as a sacred and auspicious milky white elephant, revered in *Hinduism, Buddhism,* and *Jainism*[22]. Interestingly, Indra asks for this mighty being, *Airavata*, to be his vahana (carrier). White here stands for 'sentience and clarity.' It also represents the ultimate phase in alchemy, symbolising light and oneness.

Let's delve deeper into the 'alchemical aspect' of *Airavata*. What does it really mean for him to emerge from the ocean as a fully white elephant? It is not so much the colour and the skin tone, but the moving from the *nigredo*, the darkness—the shadow work in the depths of our own psyche. Only then does he emerge from the oceanic realm, being bathed in the milky white ocean.

One must go through all the phases of the alchemical process and evolve. It's important not to reduce dark to being bad and white to good but as the alchemical property of moving from shadow to light. In this context, white symbolises alchemy and can be seen as divine. It is imperative for us to contemplate. What does it truly mean, beyond the literal colour?

When I first started studying symbolism, I found myself perplexed by the choice of the mighty elephant as Indra's vahana (carrier). Yet, as I reflect on the years of soul-searching and self-transformation, I am convinced that he is the ideal choice for Indra, the Rain God. *Airavata's* relation to rain and fertility makes it the very source of life, thereby ushering in prosperity to Mother Nature, helping humans and other species thrive.

Imagine the consequences if we do not have rain, as we witnessed last summer in Bengaluru, Karnataka. Usually, Bengaluru receives an abundance of rain by this time, but it did not start until May 2024, leaving us to suffer in the scorching heat. This was especially unbearable because we have been spoiled by cool temperatures and regular rainfall in Bengaluru, signifying climate change.

It highlights the importance of our connection to nature and raises the question of why we engage in activities such as plundering, cutting down massive trees, and depleting our green spaces and habitats—amid growing climate change concerns. While growth is undoubtedly important, we must consider the consequences and how it impacts other species. Because of this unchecked growth, it is truly distressing to hear about numerous rail accidents and the tragic deaths of elephants. Thankfully, artificial intelligence is now being utilised to address this issue.

Sacred Connection to Nature

Growing up in *Malnad*[23], we were taught beautiful songs that instilled a connection to nature. This particular song goes like this: *huyo huyo maleraya, mavina totake nirilla*, which translates to 'please rain, the mango orchard needs your blessings.'

In the year 2019 as well, Bengaluru experienced a late onset of the monsoon. Just before it started, I was teaching my niece this song, explaining how it could help invoke the rain gods. While I don't consider myself a magician or a shaman, it rained. It was just me bringing the right kind of feeling state. It is crucial to educate children about interconnectedness and being in synchrony with nature.

Now, with the persistent floods, we must seriously consider what we are doing to our own home and planet. It is wonderful to worship, give labels and titles, and celebrate festivals, but how do we instil these values in ourselves and our children?

This is where *Airavata* comes into play. I remember being mesmerised by the beautiful and striking image of *Airavata* carrying Indra and his wife. They appeared to be one unit as they traversed the universe. The loyalty *Airavata* shows to Indra teaches us about love, friendship and devotion to ourselves and others. This loyalty goes beyond utilitarianism; it represents a deeper connection. In fact, many species thrive due to elephants, which is why they are often known as the *'gardeners of the forest.'*

In what aspects of your life do you experience this deep connection and unwavering loyalty? If not, where will you begin? Start by taking a moment to reflect, then proceed with small, steady steps.

Understanding Airavata and Anima Mundi

We will now examine the mesmerising and mysterious cosmology of 'Mount Meru' found in various Asian traditions. The mountain is said to be the *unus-mundus*—*'centre of the universe'*, with four faces representing divinities, adorned with precious gems and supported by four majestic elephants. *Airavata*, one of the celestial elephants, holds the mountain in the east—the direction of the rising sun. This key role also includes *guarding our universe.*

Whether or not one believes in the existence of this cosmic mountain, it holds profound symbolism. It can represent our inner mountain and compass, reflecting the microcosm within the macrocosm. By connecting with *Airavata* as an inner archetypal figure, alongside its outer manifestation, it can serve as an *inner guide* and *guru* (teacher). This association allows us to delve deeper into our rich spiritual history.

How can we emulate *Airavata* and embody the attributes that lead to a wholesome life and self-realisation? What qualities should we strive to develop as ideals?

Ultimately, what is *Airavata* guiding us towards? Who is *Airavata* to you at this juncture?

We all know that *Airavata* is the divine white elephant. Now, let's understand and explore why *Airavata* is Indra's vahana (carrier). Is he symbolising an ideal mahout (elephant caretaker)? Could this be similar to some of the best elephant-mahout pairs known? Moreover, I wonder how Elephant Leela, my little one, immediately took to me even though I am not her mahout. This is perhaps more of a longing, a longing for the mother from whom she was sadly separated and captured at a young age. I do not give her commands, yet she follows me like a child.

In Jungian terms, we say that it is the projection of the mother (or father) archetype that aids in recreating the bond/connection, which is also the primary aim of therapy—to bring about a shift, healing and transformation through reconnections.

When a senior mahout was told about my connection to Leela, he shared a story of how he had bonded with the elephant in his charge, as they both grew up together from a young age. It is beautiful to witness their interactions and the mutual understanding they have, even without words. His words deeply resonated with me, "Some elephants just take to you immediately." I felt accepted as someone who sincerely understands elephants, as it is the heart-to-heart connections that matter—Elephants truly see your soul. The purpose of this association is entirely to support those elephants who are amongst humans, without endorsing captivity.

Akin to the *Sonepur mela*, there are unfortunate instances of illegal capturing of wild elephant calves for the purpose of trading captive elephants. These incidents are still reported in a few locations in the northeast, along the Assam-Arunachal and Assam-Nagaland border (Bhaskaran et al, 2011, Varma & Kumar 2010).

Airavata can be seen as an archetype signifying the inner guide. The divine being guiding us to fulfil our divine purpose in this earthly sojourn, firstly, by working on ourselves and perhaps inspiring others.

"What makes some connections, including those of animal workers, so special and a joy to watch? I feel it is the time taken to really bond and understand the other. Also, it could mirror the light, the work (process) and our divine magnificence. A thought I urge you to ponder, wonder and reflect or even play with."

What does the animal perceive? What was the relation and equation between Indra and *Airavata* that made *Airavata* immensely loyal? He brought rain, fought for him, stood his ground, and guarded when Indra was in trouble. What motivates the elephant to do this? It is not simply following commands; there appears to be a deeper mystery. How connected the mahouts are within themselves? Do the mahouts reflect and do the inner work? We will explore this further in the next section.

I know when I am shaky, Elephant Leela is going to be shaky. When mahouts are jittery, it shows in their body language, in the 'energetic field', and the elephants are going to pick up that energy. We have witnessed many occasions when there's anxiety in the space; it is clearly mirrored, seen and sensed by the elephants. Whereas even when they are feeling anxious and triggered, if the person in charge remains calm and composed, the elephant will sense this and gradually mirror their state and relax.

In psychology, this is known as 'mirroring,' where we aim to instil the state we want, in this case, a sense of calmness. For example, when an athlete is tense, simply telling them to calm down is not enough. It is important to help them relax and to mirror that relaxation in myself. This significantly benefits the athlete and the field.

I even apply this approach with our elephants. The way I am, my body language, prosody (tone)—all of it, is sensed by the elephants, and it helps establish a sense of connection and safety. When I gently stroke their trunks, reassuring them, like with Leela, saying, "It's okay, and I am here." It has proven to be effective in assisting with the transition of Leela to another centre as well. However, it is not always as easy for another elephant that I had not yet established a strong connection. There have been multiple occasions when the elephants have reciprocated by holding me, especially when I am feeling down or unwell. Their presence has had the power to bring about a positive shift in my well-being.

Image Source: Bhimbetka rock shelters (UNESCO World Heritage Site in Madhya Pradesh)

The Airavata Archetype and Elephant Well-being

Sri Krishna, in the *Bhagavad Gita*[24], says, "I am *Airavata* among the elephants."—exalting his divinity.

What would the archetype of *Airavata* hold, especially in today's world?

Currently, to whom are we loyal? Are we loyal and connected to our own selves, to life around us, and to the mysteries of what is? On what basis is this loyalty? Is it blunt or has it been handed down? Have I reflected upon it? What am I giving my time and energy to? Is it nourishing my soul? Is it helping the larger collective? Is it helping me delve into my own inner depths/soul?

My Jungian trainer had asked me, "if animals possess a consciousness and if the elephant minds doing what it's been asked to do." When I was discussing certain practices deeply ingrained in our culture, while also holding elephant well-being in mind. This perspective has really helped me hold all angles.

Now, when I observe certain spaces, camps, rituals and the cultural ethos, I first consider the nature of the *space*. What is the equation between the elephant, the mahout and the system? Similar to the relationship between an athlete and the whole sporting ecosystem. I am examining the system at play here.

A mahout may still have his stick, but does he use it? The more I have observed mahouts and elephants in various settings, I often wonder, what is the association. This attunement is something we will explore further in the next section. The relational field is key to the elephants, and our own understanding of the elephant.

What really is the elephant and mahout pair?

What really is the elephant here?

What really is the king of elephants, the 'elephantine spirit', speaking to us, showing us at this point in time when society is so deeply disconnected from life, from our own inner core self?

Jung talks of the exchange between a learned scholar and an old man who asks the scholar how he was, and the scholar says, as he can see, he is learned and successful. To which the old man asks if he was happy and fully alive since he saw him lecture and the scholar appeared anxious to judgement. Hence, was restless, hasty, and not in himself. The scholar knew it was right, though he did not pay heed to it at first (Pg. 256, Red Book).

Guess this is the narrative of the current age to run behind fame and glory at the cost of oneself. Then life throws certain challenges that make us look at it closely and prioritise how we'd like to live. Are we pursuing what we are passionate about and adding value to life? This is a good starting point, although there are other potential paths to consider as well.

What does *Airavata* represent to you, beyond being a magnificent elephant, a white, majestic, divine elephant, along with his wife, *Abhramu*, from whom the elephant ancestry seems to have begun? What is he saying to you? What do we need as a collective society to restore *Airavata* and his race to their rightful place and give them the 'rights of passage' (Menon et al, 2005) by preserving their remaining habitats?

This is what I am sitting with and holding. I am hoping to get more messages and dreams and, as a collective, may we be guided by many more.

I genuinely believe the elephant space is so much more evolved than us. It was an emotion I had long held. Then I happened to read about the Zoological classification of Africans who hold the elephants first on the evolutionary ladder. Then comes lions, and humans are much later, indicating that we really are a younger race. Is that why the elephants are being tolerant of us?

On the contrary, we are now at the cost of wreaking havoc on our own planet, Mother Earth.

May we be guided by the wisdom of *Airavata* as we move through these challenging times and look at what is the opportunity here. We need to hold the intention, hope, and be open to their wisdom and blessings.

As we come towards the end of the chapter, I want to bring this interesting folklore connected to *Mahabharata*[25], which says that "*Arjuna*[26] brought down the celestial elephant to earth, so his mother could worship him." The story goes that *Gandhari*[27], representing the *Kauravas*[28], conducted a religious ceremony worshipping elephants made of clay or gold but ignored *Kunti*[29] for it. To please his mother, Arjuna prays to his divine father Indra to send his loyal mount. *Airavata* then peeps through the cloud, and it is said Arjuna creates a stairway with his arrows for the divine elephant to descend to earth, and the arduous task of ensuring the arrows were held strong for the mighty giant.

Such a powerful allegory for work, patience and devotion to beseech the divine *Airavata* into our lives and worship him. Also, a poignant message to spare the real elephants to be free in their natural habitat and to stop glamorising captivity.

I conclude this chapter with this thought on their sacredness:

"Brahma concealed in each of the animals a profound secret. The secret of the mystic syllables, *amsvara,* he concealed in the horse.

In the Elephant '... a beast of the moon with crescent tusks, who has emerged from the churning of the seas...', Brahma said, "He concealed wisdom."—Sacred Elephant (Heathcote Williams, p.8).

Can we find guidance in *Airavata*, our inner compass, as we embark on our journey within to discover our divine self? By doing so, we can experience a profound sense of joy that radiates outward.

The arrival of elephants in my life has brought a newfound richness, their compassionate presence filling my days. Serving these magnificent creatures has been a deeply soulful experience. May you too be touched by their energy, blossoming, and feeling a profound interconnectedness with all of life.

* * *

Reflections

1. What is the first image of Airavata that comes to you?
2. Where do you think he is pointing?
3. Invite his guidance and watch your dreams.
4. What is the energy of this archetype that you could call into your life for a deeper connection to yourself and others?

Notes

1. **Vahana**: Vehicle or carrier used by deities in Hinduism.
2. **Diggaja**: Elephants of the four quarters symbolising the guardians of the directions.
3. **CS**: Author's initials.
4. **Space**: Refers to the energetic field in metaphysical contexts.
5. **Brahma**: The creator god in Hinduism, part of the Trimurti, along with Vishnu and Shiva.
6. **Field**: Refers to the energetic or psychological space in psychology, where interactions between individuals and their environment occur.
7. **Ramayana**: Ancient Indian epic narrating the story of Lord Rama.
8. **Iravati**: A prominent Indian river, now known as the Ravi River.

9. **Kashyapa**: One of the revered ancient sages, considered a progenitor of many beings in Hinduism.
10. **Shiva**: One of the Trimurtis, known as the destroyer and transformer in Hinduism.
11. **Garuda**: A legendary bird, depicted as the vehicle of Lord Vishnu, representing speed and martial prowess.
12. **Malasars**: An ancient tribe of elephant-keepers native to southern India.
13. **Jainu Kurubas**: Another ancient tribe of elephant-keepers, traditionally found in the forests of South India.
14. **Pataloka**: The underworld realm in Hindu cosmology, often described as being below the earth.
15. **Vishnu Purana**: A major mediaeval text in Hinduism detailing the history and cosmology associated with Lord Vishnu.
16. **Dhurvasa**: A revered sage known for his temper and role in various Hindu legends.
17. **Lakshmi**: Goddess of wealth, fortune and prosperity, and consort of Lord Vishnu.
18. **Trimurti**: The triad of three principal gods in Hinduism—Brahma (the creator), Vishnu (the preserver), and Shiva (the destroyer).
19. **Krishna**: An incarnation of Vishnu and a central figure in the *Mahabharata*, known for his teachings in the *Bhagavad Gita*.
20. **Kurma Avatar**: The second avatar of Vishnu, taking the form of a tortoise to support Mount Mandara during the churning of the ocean.
21. **Samudra Manthan**: The churning of the ocean, a legendary event involving gods and demons in pursuit of the nectar of immortality.
22. **Hinduism, Buddhism & Jainism**: The ancient Indian religions and traditions.
23. **Malnad**: A hilly region in Karnataka, India, known for its dense forests and diverse wildlife.
24. **Bhagavad Gita**: A revered Hindu scripture that is part of the *Mahabharata*, consisting of Lord Krishna's teachings to Arjuna.

25. **Mahabharata**: An ancient Indian epic, one of the longest poems in the world, depicting the Kurukshetra War and philosophical teachings.
26. **Arjuna**: A master archer and warrior prince from the *Mahabharata*, known for his role in the epic's central battle.
27. **Gandhari**: Mother of the Kauravas in the *Mahabharata*, known for blindfolding herself as an act of solidarity with her blind husband.
28. **Kauravas**: The antagonistic group of cousins in the *Mahabharata* who fought against the Pandavas in the Kurukshetra War.
29. **Kunti**: The mother of the Pandavas in the *Mahabharata*, known for her unwavering devotion and strength.

"We inherited wonder. Let us not leave behind only regret."

Chapter 2

GANESHA ~ THE ALCHEMICAL GOD

"*Let* us put our hands together, invoke *Ganesha*[1], and seek the blessings of the elephant-headed God. The Lord of the *Ganas*[2], first to be worshipped, remover of obstacles, bestower of boons, the god of new beginnings.

With his childlike innocence and exuberant smile, he delights our minds and gladdens our hearts. Born to the Goddess, he loses his human head and is born anew with the mighty elephant's head. A perfect nature being—with a human body and elephant head guiding humans to a state of wholeness. The divine child from the perfect blend of *Shiva*[3] and *Shakti*[4]. Let us bow our heads and seek his wisdom that he graciously bestows upon us."—CS.

Ganesha is in the space today. I would like to begin with a compelling question: Why an elephant's head?

This has always been my thought! The song *Ganappa, Ganappa*[5] comes to mind. This was cooking in the divine month of *Ganesha Chaturthi*[6] and finally began to flow just after we finished the celebrations. The most poignant aspect of this festival is how we must learn to 'let go' of what we have brought in with so much love, taken care, and then need to let go of *Ganesha* during the *visarjan*[7] (immersion). In ancient times, Lord *Ganesha*, also known as *Ganapati*, was crafted out of clay or red mud, symbolising how he came into being.

It was *Goddess Parvati's*[8] essence that birthed *Ganesha*, at least the first form. The song: *Ganapathy bapa mauriya, jaldi aa thu agle sal* which translates into 'hail Lord Ganesha, please come early next year'. This is reminiscent of my *Ajji's* (grandmother) yearly farewell, where she'd urge me to return early for the next holiday. Watching a video of a young girl crying uncontrollably at the *Ganesha* idol's immersion brought it all back to me.

Our culture is truly beautiful, and the spirit of festivals, such as the *Ganesha* festival, is both symbolic and deep. I have a distinct memory that comes to mind—a moment when I was fascinated by the song *"Ganesha Banda"*. This song captures the essence of the festival perfectly. It goes like this: *Ganesha Banda, Hote Mele Gandah, Kai*

Kadbutinda, Chik Kerele Bidah, Dod Kerele Yeda. The lyrics carry a meaningful message, depicting Ganesha's arrival with sandalwood paste adorning his stomach, relishing his favourite treat, the delicious *ladoos (Indian sweet)* known as *kadbu* in Karnataka. The song then portrays *Ganesha* immersing himself in a smaller lake, only to emerge in the vastness of the bigger ocean.

What is the significance of this?

We bring in the idol and invoke his energy. He springs to life, but we need to let him go to the smaller lake. He emerges in *Kailasha*[9], which is known as 'the abode of his parents.'

Perhaps this is our journey, too. Alluding that at some point in time, we will have to let go of what we hold dear, including our lives and those we love. Perhaps, they disperse our *astis* (ashes) into the holy water or Mother Earth, and thus, we become one with the Divine.

Ganesha poses the question, "What in you that needs to die to be reborn?" We will delve further into this aspect, similar to a hero's journey.

I remember as a young girl, observing my grandmother and being drawn to certain rituals during the festivals. Blessings are given in the *Bagina*[10] (offering), the case is made of natural materials and called *Mara*[11] which is gifted along with a token (cash). Melodies and expressions of love and good wishes beautifully accomplish this. In this case, my granny would sing, "Please take the *bhagina, gaurama - gaurama, gaurama bagina thogolama.*"

Gaurama is the individual who's being bestowed the blessing, representing *Gauri, Ganesha's* mother. The daughter accepts the case and says, *"savitrama, savitrama, bagina thogondnama"* meaning "Yes, I receive your blessing."

In Karnataka, in particular, we call the festival *'Gauri Ganesha'*, not just Ganesha Chaturthi. The Goddess Gauri is invoked on the first day, followed by Ganesha on the next day. It is believed that *Ganesha* comes to escort his mother back to Kailasha, which is why she sheds tears while leaving her maternal home. Thereby, the rainfall is referred to as *'Gauri Malle'*, which translates to the tears of the Goddess falling from the sky.

I resonated with the ritual and would insist my grandmother should do the same with me. We were additionally given a little token to buy sweets from the elders, a kind gesture to make the farewell bearable.

Till date, this is followed in Malnad when they give cash along with the *Kumkum*[12]—a mini blessing to behold. My grandmother would also pack savoury for me, which I would finish up on the way to Bengaluru. Food is nourishment and signifies the great mother, and to me it was a way of holding on to my grandmother's loving energy.

Ganesha's belly also resembles the earth and the ability to digest food. The experiences along with the challenges that are bound to come up in life.

Have we wondered why we like to feast during festivals—perhaps a longing for deep nourishment and the great mother?

Jungian Analyst, Marion Woodman explained that most eating disorders allude to this longing, and a rupture in early childhood shows up in relation to food. I am sure we all have felt the need to binge or starve during intense emotional periods, too.

In addition, let's consider the healing power of tears and the connection to rain. In today's age, we are told to be strong and not cry, especially like a girl. Perhaps a woman's gentleness is the source of her strength in childbirth, regardless of species. Women also bleed (menstruate) every month and release—a kind of rebirth. No wonder it is called 'moon time'—signifying the connection between the moon and waters. We will explore these aspects further as we go deeper into the book.

Ganesha's Birth

Let us delve into this lesser-known version of his birth. Shiva and Parvati are the divine couple and lead a blissful life. Shiva, being an ascetic, would go into meditation and the upkeep of the world for extended ages. Parvati occasionally longed for company. While bathing in the Ganges (holy river), she gets an idea. The Goddess removes her essence and plunges it into the Ganges, and out comes this humongous, mammoth being.

Later, he's brought into a more human form. They spend their time together joyfully. One eventful day, when Shiva returns home, *Ganesha* blocks him from entering his own house because Parvati has instructed him not to allow anyone inside whilst bathing.

This is, in my opinion, a crucial place to pause and assess what was actually happening here. Notice, both the masculine, the young masculine in *Ganesha* and the divine masculine Shiva are at loggerheads and end up in a battle. Evidently, Shiva is unaware that this is his own child, given birth by Parvati alone. Because he was not part of the process, he didn't acknowledge the intruder. *Ganesha* initially, out of respect for his mother, but at a later point, more of stubbornness, refuses entry to the Lord of the house.

In the battle, Shiva in his fury beheads *Ganesha*. The Goddess is grief stricken, and the whole universe goes into bareness. Brahma and the rest of the gods bring a truce for the well-being of the planet. Shiva agrees and asks to 'bring the head of the first creature in the Northern direction.'

Is it synchronous that it's the elephant head that is then placed on *Ganesha*, thus imbuing him with life, giving him the name '*Gajanana*'— one with an elephant face?

When we view it from a symbolic lens, the masculine was missing, the divine masculine essence of Shiva, had to be integrated. That's when *Ganesha* becomes fully embodied as the Divine Child, from the union of the God Shiva and Goddess in the *Devi*[13], a symbol of wholeness and oneness (Ravitz, 1995), therefore worshiped first, particularly prior to any new venture.

Only when he is reborn, *Ganesha* is granted the boon of being the first worshipped in the Hindu pantheon.

Thus, if we go into the meaning of each line and ponder on it, there is much to learn. Importantly, the elephant is the largest land mammal, yet gentle unless provoked. Not to forget their intelligence mirrored in *Ganesha's* lores, too.

In turn, favouring him to be *Vyasa's*[14] choice for a scribe, he wrote non-stop. The great epic *Mahabaratha* was completed with *Ganesha's* involvement!

The story unfolds as follows. Vyasa wished to undertake writing the grand epic. He invokes *Ganesha*, who lays a condition that the dictation must be uninterrupted; only then will he undertake the venture. In light of the challenge, Vyasa accepts and suggests Ganesha to write only on understanding each stanza.

Vyasa would dictate intricate verses at a stretch whenever he needed a break; the young deity would then spend some time deciphering them before writing them.

Such was *Ganesha's* prudence that upon breaking his pen, he used a tusk instead, and that's why his iconic image with a broken tusk. The deeper meaning is wholeness in imperfection, despite the broken tusk.

A wonderful message indeed, especially considering our high expectations for perfection. But, is it really possible to achieve perfection in everything, all the time? What is the price we have to pay? Perhaps we risk losing our sense of self and become robotic.

What's coming up in you right now? I urge you to jot down any thoughts, images or ideas as you read along as they are messages of your inner world!

Remover of Obstacles

It's no surprise *Ganesha* is called V*ignaharaka*—'the remover of obstacles.'

Even during Ganesha Chaturthi, it is told that when Lord *Ganesha* is being led for his visarjan (immersion), *Ganesha* removes the obstacles in our path and ushers in blessings. I do not intend to avoid work, but instead to ask for support and guidance in the undertaking, whatever that may be. For example, when I broke my foot, my house help suggested intending prayers to our family deity. Along with it, I had to work on my rehabilitation and build myself. I feel that's where the impact is perhaps stronger and faster.

I find the true spirit of festivities and deities beautiful and touching. But one wonders if we are now emulating the essence of what is actually happening? Nowadays, it seems to be all pomp and show. The ritual has lost its meaning with the outward show but rarely inward action. There was a point where paint was used for *Ganesha murtis* (idols), sadly polluting the water bodies. Even during the visarjan, the crowds or some mischief mongers, cause havoc, leading to mishaps.

I heard that a couple celebrated the occasion grandly, and the lady had decorated expensive jewellery on the deity. However, they overlooked it during the visarjan and had to drain all the water to retrieve the jewellery. It is the purity of your service, your *aradhana* (devotion) that appeases *Ganesha*, perhaps gone missing here.

Celebrations are essential to stay connected/bond and build a sense of community. We also need to be in tune with the rhythms of life and our spiritual self—wholeness as *Ganesha* symbolises. It's important to dress up, enjoy good food, and have fun, while also being mindful of our impact on nature and others.

There is a boy's hostel near my house, and we noticed they fire *patakas* (firecrackers) all the time for every festival, victory and now I feel for no reason. One day I was coming back home, and someone burst the crackers very close to our vehicle. I think if the window was open, one of us could have gotten hurt.

I find myself wondering, are we genuinely taking a moment to pause? Are we truly reflecting? Are we connecting with ourselves and with nature by pondering on the essence of this festival and the deity it represents? What is this deity signifying? What are we doing?

Our actions seem to be contradictory. Unfortunately, this is disheartening because we are actively polluting the environment—the land, air and waters. Specifically, we are contaminating the rivers. Astonishingly, we even believe that immersing painted idols symbolises our successful celebration of the festival. At one point, authorities prohibited the immersion of idols in the lakes of Bengaluru due to the resulting pollution and chaos. Hopefully, this led to a shift in attitudes and actions.

Thankfully, we now see more eco-friendly practices. Some time ago, I learned about chocolate *Ganesha*. After the festival, the chocolate melts and is distributed to children nearby. I was impressed by this concept, as it allows us to contribute to society and be environmentally conscious at the same time!

Do we project our shadow on others? Perhaps a point to think about. A segment in the subsequent section is devoted to shadow work.

In the year 2024, an artist in Tamil Nadu displayed the Wayanad miracle story with 'Elephants protecting an old lady and her grandchild during the raging floods', signifying the forest protectors standing guard for the humans until help arrived.

What really is the significance of the festival? How would *Ganesha* feel? I often wonder the same about elephants being held captive at institutions. Have we lost the meaning of customs?

I recall seeing an 'elephant blessing' throughout the morning and at times in the hot sun to garland a VIP, with no respite to relish fodder or fruits that lay close to her. The elephant looked dissociated—repeating the action, which had no meaning to her. I sat motionless, too akin to her state/plight. It impacted me, but I stayed with her and broke down on coming back to the hotel.

Solitary captivity or keeping hordes of elephants together in chains leads to stress and psychological issues such as head bobbing and swaying. There are also more serious issues that can be traumatic and result in both human and elephant casualties. Not to forget the well-documented physical issues such as foot problems and diabetes.

Next time you hear of an elephant gone crazy, please ask 'what was it bearing so long that it lost its cool?'

Though I could see the enthusiasm of the crowd, it was momentary. But what about the elephant bound to a place, when as a species they are meant to roam and nourish the forest?

Animal communicators say that elephants raise the energy of the place and the vibration of the planet. How wonderful it is when they can do so in their natural habitat. Animal lovers and elephant workers are encouraging 'robotic elephants' that can hold a fascination and even bless.

As I am writing this very section, I received a video where a biker ventures close to an elephant group with a calf. He was lucky to escape alive with a mock charge. Honestly, what else could this be if not stupidity? Any mishap would have been blamed on the elephant.

Our so-called intelligent species of humans can surely be sensitive and show some respect by maintaining distance in their shrinking habitats.

Embodying Nature

Another aspect I wanted to explore is *Ganesha* being considered a 'perfect nature being'. The *Puranas* describe him as the blend of human and animal, depicting man's eternal striving towards nature, hinting at the world soul.

Can you guess the reason? Let's look at how many beings are there in our exuberant *Ganesha*?

One can't forget the elephant head, then his vahana (carrier) is the mouse, or what we call *mushika*[15]. He also has a snake tied around the waist, while the fourth is the human body, or the human being.

When you observe it in this manner, it's symbolically pointing to focus as much on our instinct, our actions (doing), and to the wild, to the raw, to the human as well as the animal. Therefore, to give every element and every being its place under the sun. Perhaps that's why we find a multitude of species in nature, each with its own specific role and place. Any wonder, a mere glimpse of Ganesha brings us joy, perhaps an ancient calling to strive towards nature!

When we consider life from this perspective, is it fair to ignore the symbolism and over-focus on man alone? As it is happening in our world now.

What symbol or metaphor is more fitting than *Ganesha* himself?

Ganesha with an elephant head has the mouse as his vahana and Indra has the elephant as his vahana, as we saw in the last chapter. Whilst the elephant clears and makes pathways in the forest, the little mouse scurries underground. Both are needed to clear the path and make way. Hence, rightly, called the 'remover of obstacles'. But sadly, their own 'pathways' have been fragmented and degraded by us.

Creativity and Boredom

"What did you do as a child that made the hours pass like minutes? Herein lies the key to your earthly pursuits."

– **Carl Jung**

How is creativity born? In this age of overdoing, if one doesn't pause, there is no scope for creativity.

If you remember, Parvati sought something more. It was that spark, that thought, which then gave her the idea of hurling her body essence or *haldi* (turmeric) into the Ganges. Thus, birthing *Ganesha* through her *Shakti* (essence).

With the power of intention and through the amalgamation of earth and water, the magic happened. The creative potential is sparked. Probably the reason, *Ganesha's* energy is sought in all creative endeavours, as he is the patron of art and writing.

Isn't it alchemical? Then, of course, the Shiva, the masculine, had to come in through the head, with the elephant head signifying the instinct too.

How often do we actually pause and reflect on the deeper meanings?

After finishing writing some parts of the book, I felt the need for some alone time. An event came up, and I had to attend along with various other things. Eventually, I had to prioritise my well-being and decline to take on additional tasks. I really needed the time to go blank, enter the void, and then, in that stillness, something churns and births. That's how my creativity works. For someone else, it could be in another way.

Even during my talk preparations, I like to play with ideas. I enjoy brainstorming with mind maps; this helps me organise my thoughts and gain clarity. If you look at the whole book as well, that's how it has been written.

The alchemical creation requires us to take the time and effort for the emergence and birthing of a project akin to the physical birthing.

I'd urge you to reflect on how I give myself that time and space to create something in this age where we are bombarded with stimuli. Can I make time to switch off my phone? Is it okay if I shut down, clean, or do nothing?

I remember taking my young niece to the farm, and while I was talking to our caretaker, she said, "I am bored." I said, "Oh, that's good." I indicated the presence of greenery here and a small bird there and added "just start noticing." Again, she said, "Oh, I am so bored, Tavi (the name she gave me). I don't know what to do." I said, "It's good to get bored." She looked at me like I didn't get her. Once I got busy with work, she figured out a way—found sticks and started playing by creating in sand.

Isn't that what we all want? Natural spaces open up a child, not just children but even us. Sometimes, I can sit for hours together just by a water body, or an ocean, a lake, or any natural space, and be one with the space/environment. We need to allow ourselves to just be and tune into life at times, at least!

Unsurprisingly, when I just keep doing too much; at a point, my body starts showing it in different ways through small aches and pains. I even zone out, and that's a signal that I am just not functioning, and my irritability levels begin to soar. If we don't listen, then the body will find a way to get our attention by putting on some breaks!

As a society, we have undoubtedly experienced growth, but it is crucial to question the price we have paid for it.

Furthermore, what about the stillness and the contentment of our ancestors? I used to feel this contentment with my grandparents that spread to us too!

Do we need to binge-watch? Is it necessary to always be doing something?

When I tell people I just want to chill on Sunday and get the much-needed 'me time', a lot of people don't get it, but I suppose that's also a very introverted way.

Root Chakra and Abhaya Mudra

Lord *Ganesha* rules the 'root chakra', also called the *Muladhara Chakra*[16], which is associated with stability and grounding. If this chakra is balanced, a person is rooted and strong, which is essential for all aspects of life. We also see that *Ganesha* is depicted with the *Abhaya mudra*[17] signifying 'fearlessness' that is needed for a successful outcome.

The root chakra stability with the Abhaya mudra fearlessness is a great concoction for success with wisdom, the elephant's strength with the nimbleness of the mushika, innocent and wise, gleeful and reflective.

An invitation for us to probe into all aspects of ourselves and birth the new potent energy. Unity in diversity is the perfect idiom to describe the symbolism of *Ganesha*.

The image of *Ganesha* is depicted with fruits, implying to put in the hard work and enjoy the fruits. I hope we can bear at least some of these aspects in mind and get to the essence of this multifaceted deity, more than just on the festival day, but to invite his energy or hold the archetypal image to delve into our deeper self.

Similarly, may we remember the elephants and ensure their well-being throughout the year and not just during festivities such as *Dasara*[18]. Also, to celebrate the wild elephants by giving them respect and space and not just glamourise the camp or captive elephants.

I often wonder if they would want nothing more than freedom! Remember the Wayanad forest elephants who stood guard? Reports indicate this incident took place during the Wayanad landslides caused by heavy rains. Three wild elephants, including a tusker, were standing right beside a grandmother and her child, as if guarding them, throughout the entire night until help arrived. They deserve the right attention too, but from a distance!

As we draw close to this chapter, I'd like to look at the intelligence of *Ganesha* even when young. He is the child who circled 'the world' three times in his parents' abode itself to be given the special fruit. *Karthikeyan*[19], the swifter brother, takes off on his peacock vahana (carrier). *Ganesha* undeterred circumambulates his parents thrice and seeks the reward, saying the divine couple is the world to him. His spiritual insight and smartness lead to wisdom. May we develop this foresight similar to the *Ganesha*.

Hero's Journey: Initiation, Trials and Transformation

Lord *Ganesha's* journey from his birth, the trials and sacrifices with the beheading, and finally coming to his true power and becoming a leader is akin to a hero's journey. May we invoke him when we're embarking on new paths and become change-makers. This is our intent and hopes with AANE, to instil a sense of responsibility and leadership among the youth for a more inclusive world with nature at the core, not elevating humans above everything else. A Forest Officer echoed the need to involve the youth, and in addition, commended our work.

My Encounter with Lord Ganesha

At this juncture, it's apt to share my journey with *Ganesha*. As much as I love elephants, I didn't have much of a personal association with the deity growing up and couldn't fathom the various aspects of the image. It was only after the elephants came into my life and I was fascinated with symbology, did I begin to understand the deeper meaning of this deity.

When I made the bold decision to move to Australia for my PhD, I mostly received *Ganesha* figurines as a good luck charm. Now when I reflect, *Ganesha* was guiding my arduous journey in a faraway land with no friends or family. Unknowingly, folks were drawn to *Ganesha's* idols to wish me well on my journey. As satisfying as it was to obtain my doctorate from Perth, it was a journey of overcoming many obstacles.

Honestly, I am beginning to be aware of this only now as I write this section. I found myself in an unknown extroverted culture and the pressure of being the first Indian in the department, a true test of performance for a budding Sports Psychologist. Life did bring me new friends and amazing dolphins as I lived close to Swan River. I will share about the surreal experience that lasted throughout my four years in the concluding chapter.

You may not believe me, but I owe my gratitude to them and the river as well, since they held me and reconnected me to my core introverted self. I spent most evenings with the Dolphins after the human crowd subsided. Was this the beginning of my inter-species connection? We'll see in the course of the book.

Now, if you're wondering how I started my journey with *Ganesha*. Coming from a *Shaivite*[20] family, my devotion was to Shiva, then gradually the Goddess. Only during 2020, a year after the Elephants had entered my personal life, did *Gajalakshmi* (Goddess of Elephants) and *Ganesha* make their presence strong.

It was while delving deep into my Elephant symbolism talk that I truly understood the depth and significance of *Ganesha* and the Goddess (that we'll meet in section 3). Every song attributed to *Ganesha* talks of his journey and how he guides us onward on our paths.

I'd like you to pause and really sit with your own journey.

I am sure we've all met him at various junctures, even if one is not a Hindu or religious. Tune into the archetypal and see where in your life you can invoke this energy, and perhaps when it has silently guided you. I am enamoured with the nature connection being a nature lover and worshipper. What about you?

The image of *Ganesha* emerging from Parvati and the holy Ganges—the sustainer of life and his beatific development to becoming *Ganesha* is a wonderful image to hold and ponder on the heroic journey. The feminine Goddesses and his wonderful relation with the mother call us to pay attention to what needs nurturing in us.

Interestingly, the elephants are led by the matriarch too! Importantly, to also welcome Shiva - the masculine energy after which he becomes a true leader with the elephant head, symbolic of wholeness. This is a good metaphor to hold as we embark on our own calling and life path.

It is befitting to end the chapter with this quote that happens to be one of my favourites:

"Heroes are agents of change."

– Campbell.

* * *

Reflections

1. What about Ganesha draws you?
2. Which aspect of your life needs to change?
3. Are you ready to 'let go' of the old?
4. What shifts do you want to bring forth?

Notes

1. **Ganesha**: The elephant-headed Hindu deity, revered as the remover of obstacles and patron of arts, sciences and wisdom.
2. **Ganas**: The attendants of Lord Shiva, representing collective energies and symbolising Shiva's retinue.
3. **Shiva**: The father of Ganesha and a principal deity in Hinduism, known as the destroyer and regenerator in the Trimurti, complementing Ganesha's role as the remover of obstacles.
4. **Shakti**: The divine feminine energy personified as Goddess Parvati, Ganesha's mother, symbolising creation and nurturing power.
5. **Song Ganappa, Ganappa**: A devotional song celebrating Ganesha, often performed during religious rituals and festivals.
6. **Ganesha Chaturthi**: A popular Hindu festival dedicated to the birth of Ganesha, involving elaborate rituals and celebrations.
7. **Visarjan**: The immersion of Ganesha idols in water, marking the conclusion of the Ganesha Chaturthi festival.

8. **Goddess Parvati's**: The consort of Shiva and mother of Ganesha, embodying fertility, love and devotion.
9. **Kailasha**: The sacred mountain and abode of Lord Shiva and Goddess Parvati, symbolising spiritual attainment.
10. **Bagina**: A ceremonial offering in South Indian traditions, symbolising prosperity and reverence.
11. **Mara**: A bamboo tray-like design used to offer Bagina.
12. **Kumkum**: A red powder used in Hindu rituals and worn as a mark of devotion or marital status.
13. **Devi**: A term for the divine feminine, encompassing various goddesses and aspects of Shakti.
14. **Vyasa**: A legendary sage and the author of the Mahabharata, credited with compiling the Vedas.
15. **Mushika**: The mouse, which serves as the vehicle (vahana) of Ganesha, symbolising humility by overcoming obstacles.
16. **Muladhara Chakra**: The root chakra in Indian spirituality, located at the base of the spine and symbolising grounding and survival.
17. **Abhaya Mudra**: A hand gesture representing fearlessness, protection and reassurance in Indian iconography.
18. **Dasara**: A Hindu festival celebrating the victory of good over evil, associated with the story of the Goddess Durga and Ravana.
19. **Karthikeyan**: The elder son of Shiva and Parvati, a deity associated with war, wisdom and leadership.
20. **Shaivite Family**: Refers to the divine family of Lord Shiva, symbolising unity and balance.

"The most sacred offering is not in flowers or fire—but in freeing the ones who bear his form."

Chapter 3

PALAKAPYA: THE FIRST CONSERVATIONIST ~ LEGACY FOR CURRENT STATE OF ELEPHANTS

Palakapya[1] in dialogue with the mythical King *Romapada*[2]
"Formally, elephants could wander wherever they pleased and assume any shape.
They roamed as they liked in the sky and on earth...
Forest elephants that dwelled there happily,
and by the power of fate, have been brought to towns in bonds.
Afflicted by sufferings of mind and body, are unable for long to sustain life.
When from their own kind, they have come into the control of men...
Warriors only fight, horses only draw chariots,
but elephants that are fit for a king both fight and draw...
Thus, O King, having reached 120 years and
having performed many kinds of work, the elephant goes to heaven..."
(Source: *The Matangalila*[3])

King Romapada questions *Palakapya*, "So what can we do now?"

Beckons serious reflection to support and protect our own heritage species, before it is too late.

The Legend of Palakapya

Palakapya is the mythical sage, the Messiah, the Saviour of elephants credited with the *Hastaayurveda*[4]—on the upkeep of elephants.

So, what can we do now? A thought that King *Romapada* of *Anga*[5] poses to *Palakapya*. It's a pertinent question to hold even at this time.

In response to the king's question, *Palakapya* then narrates that elephants were once free and could roam and fly anywhere. But then, sadly, one of them crashes on an *irate sage* as he was listening to this sage's story, not realising that the tree wouldn't bear his weight. The sage, in a moment of misfortune, curses the entire elephant species to lose their ability to travel and be bound to earth-serving mortals. However, the elephants of the quarters that guard and hold our earth and universe were spared from the curse.

But then they were in great distress to see their kin and brethren and wondered what would happen to them when they would have to search for food, digest it, and heed their health on earth. They go to Brahma, asking him, what is the way forward. He assures them that in time, a sage will be born who is fond of elephants and adept at taking care of them.

The sage was none other than *Palakapya*.

It is said that when the elephants in heaven—from the quarters—see that their brethren are happy and being looked after well; they shower rain on earth, blessing us all.

Prajna Chowta, an elephant conservationist, draws inspiration from *Palakapya*. She even rescued two captive elephants and attempted the module to rewild them near Dubare Elephant Camp, Karnataka. As a result, the herd grew.

Unfortunately, whether it was her elephants or the wild elephants, they started entering coffee plantations, causing concerns among farmers and locals. The elephants were subsequently moved to camps.

This situation highlights the pressing issue of 'space', which conservationists are studying to address the growing concerns because of humans and elephants sharing space.

Now, I would like to introduce F. Edgerton's (1931) a linguistic scholar, translation of Matangalila, especially the conversation between Romapada and *Palakapya*, which is particularly pertinent in today's context with shrinking habitats.

Forest covers are quickly declining, leading to the fragmentation of elephant corridors. This, in turn, is causing concern, not only for elephants but results in increased negative human-elephant interaction.

Interestingly, *Palakapya* is credited to 'the elephant treatise'—the 'Hastyayurveda' to look after the well-being of these beautiful beings. I wonder if he knew we would eventually head to these times. Even the Kingdom of Anga, ruled by Romapada, continued to prosper. As it grew, forests were cut down to make way for more livestock and agriculture. It was during this growth that elephants began to come into contact with humans.

This interaction became more pronounced during droughts. Bamboo would sprout and attract elephants near human settlements, as stated in Matangalila. Unfortunately, citizens' concerns led to the capture of these elephants.

Thankfully, in the legend, *Palakapya* warns that if the elephant sheds tears, a curse will befall us. He requests Romapada to untie and release the elephants, so he can take them away to a faraway land where they will not disturb his kingdom. The wise king heeds this advice and releases the elephants.

As the last elephant was unchained, heaven drops started pouring and rain appeared like a blessing. I cannot help but wonder if these raindrops were also tears of joy shed by the elephants in the heavens, witnessing their brethren finally liberated from chains.

The Elephant in the Room

As I pen this chapter, amidst the tragic events of 2024 at Bandhavgarh National Park, Madhya Pradesh, where 10 elephants from a herd of 13–14 perished because of consuming the crops, a calf was left orphaned, separated from its mother and the remaining two elephants. The cause appears to be a combination of infected millet and the proximity of agriculture and the species. With elephants' intelligence, it's puzzling that they didn't detect the poison and its lethal nature.

I also wonder what the species would say when their land is being taken away in this manner.

A conservationist understands both perspectives, the farmer's distress over ruined crops, or worse, injury and death, and concurrently, the elephant's concern.

Can we contemplate over this concern? We could use more *Palakapya messiahs*[6], I believe.

The Elephants Walk

For those of us who have had the opportunity to witness the Elephant Walk, it's sheer grace. I am inviting you to imagine the graceful walk, gentle, barely audible to our human ear, yet they commune with the earth! What is the connection between the vibration of the elephant's walk, their movement, and the resulting impact? This is what comes to mind. Open yourself to the *field*—the space between you and the other (relational field) and what they invoke in you.

> *"The Elephants taught me how to listen to them."*
> **– Lawrence Anthony**

Now, I also want to bring in one of the most narrated—'the Elephant Whisperer' by Lawrence Anthony. This is the book I picked up right after the elephants made their way into my inner world.

It beautifully depicts Anthony's journey. He goes on to rehabilitate a wild herd, which would have been killed because they were too aggressive. The herd's matriarch and her calf were shot down, and the tribe witnessed this tragedy. How could they trust humans?

Thus, the next in line, along with the entire herd, were extremely stressed and anxious. They keep trying to move away from the safety of his reserve due to distrust. But he sits guard, of course, from a distance, and tries to communicate that this is a safe place to settle. Finally, the matriarch understands, calms down, and the herd is saved after a few days of tension. They made it home and developed a beautiful bond.

So, how did an animal lover do this miracle?

You will see it in the Leela chapter as well, though she is not a wild one. How did I build the connection? Or how does a mahout who is deeply connected, like the Malasars or Jainu Kurubas, form that bond with the elephant in their charge?

It's a question I have sat with for a very long time, and I am quite certain that it is through authentic connections.

More recently, Senior Jungian Analyst Marian Dunlea—the creator of body dreaming, explained that the first step in therapy is social engagement, to be fully present to the other with whatever they are feeling, to attune to the other, to the space, and allow the magic to emerge.

This is what I did with Leela, mirroring what I imagine Lawrence Anthony's approach. The Elephant Whisperer is a must-read, and when you play back that scene, it echoes Jung's quote: *"Out of chaos comes creation, out of disorder comes order."*

Even when we see an elephant settling into a new sanctuary space, it is stressful and traumatic in the beginning, but then the healing gradually happens.

The Elephant Conundrum

It is also important to know what is happening to the species and the current state of affairs. So that we can go beyond the culling, beyond the trophy hunting. In our own land, thankfully, we don't have these two, at least now, but the ivory craze, illegal captures, the disrespectful safaris of tourists chasing, posing, hurting wildlife, and worse, the industry, which has become more of entertainment in the name of culture abusing captive elephants terribly.

The earth's largest land mammal being reduced to play tricks, to do yoga, to pose in ridiculous ways are a few to name.

A friend sent me a video and suggested, "Why don't you (AANE) group raise an issue about this?"

The video showed a place in South India, where the elephant is in a pool. The elephant is made to sit down on its knees, which is not normal for elephants. Then, a non-Indian elderly gentleman struggles to sit on the elephant, and the elephant is made to spray water through the trunk. Sadly, all this is money-making and merry-making for humans, but what about the elephant?

If the elephant moves or shakes, the person risks breaking a bone or facing a life-altering situation. Merriment at the risk of injury and death?

I enquire, what brings joy in this, at the cost of another and themselves?

When Romapada asks, "What can we do now?" He's holding the welfare of his kingdom, and *Palakapya* is wondering what's going to happen to the elephants currently in captivity.

I believe there should be a merger of the two. Yes, we need to grow as a society. Honestly, if we are considered an intelligent species, we ought to be able to respect and hold the well-being of the forest and other animals. Every creature, every being, has a purpose, a reason for existing, and that purpose could benefit us too if nothing else.

We're going to be talking more about it in the sacred elephants' chapter, so we can move from *HEC to HECo-Ex*, which is from 'human-elephant conflict' to 'human-elephant co-existence.'

The Karnataka Forest Department held a conference in 2024, celebrating World Elephant Day. A conservationist from Assam explained his approach and remarked that "Co-existence is possible". The landscape was one of the areas facing human-elephant negative interaction/conflict, and that gave us hope.

Co-existence: A Possibility

Can we shift our focus towards co-existence?

How do we do this? Is it possible? Is it a dream? Do we want this? And if we don't, to ask ourselves, why not?

Let me discuss the case of the elephant calf, Bani, in a moment. However, I would first want to mention Chinnathambi, who was moved to another region, but this did not resolve the problem. In fact, it resulted in him wandering into areas that were more heavily populated by humans, and this had not occurred before. This goes to show that simply shifting and relocating animals is not the solution.

We will explore these nuances in more detail in the final section.

I want this segment to bring in these concerning aspects so that you start reflecting on them. I am sure animal lovers worldwide had bated breaths about the calf, as a herd of elephants had crossed a railway track, and sadly we lost a few of them because of the collision. A young calf was hit hard and left immobile, then rescued by an Indian non-profit organisation. Bani, the name given to the calf, is a beacon of grit; I find myself becoming quite emotional as I write this.

I contemplate the purpose of this little being—the calf, facing such a challenging fate. Days passed with doubt regarding her survival, recovery and ability to stand. This was crucial because if she couldn't stand, her life would be in jeopardy. Elephants are heavy-bodied, and when they can't stand, it will start affecting the organs. But she is now slowly but steadily walking.

I think, with Artificial Intelligence (AI), there is hope for the detection of elephant movement, but we still have a long way to go. These are ancient pathways, and elephants continue to use them.

When we don't pay heed and focus on the entirety, this is the tragic consequence affecting other species. Just as we wouldn't build a railway track on an inclined road due to obvious complications, we ought to be concerned about elephant pathways.

Just a while ago, I came across the news that the Karnataka government has restricted access to certain pathways and prohibited night travel in wildlife zones. Foremost, it is important to note that the pathway and land in question have been specifically designated for forests and wild animals. Therefore, it is imperative that no movement takes place in this area after 6 pm. If we truly value our wildlife and the beauty of nature, I am certain we can support these essential conservation measures, rather than whine about our occasional inconvenience.

When and why did we become so individualistic?

India is a collective society. Have we forgotten what it is to hold and care for each other? This care extends not only to families and friends, your animal companions but also the space, the land, including the wild animals.

Where are they going to go if we take away everything?

There was a heart-wrenching video that showed a little calf being separated from the herd and its mother in Kerala. The calf was clinging desperately to a big bus. Kudos to the driver and the conductor, who drove very slowly so that the calf would not get hurt. However, even in this situation, some people on the bus were hooting and showing no empathy for the lost child.

Its young calf and elephants take such good care of their young ones. The *allomothers* who are the aunts and the older females also provide protection. Sadly, we humans are being indifferent and hooting!

Honestly, how can anyone not feel the despair of that child? And if an infant doesn't touch our hearts, I wonder what will?

Then, as the bus departed, the calf followed behind a car. The first and sensible thing is to inform the forest department immediately. Thankfully, the calf received the help it needed from the department.

As heartbreaking as it was, energetically I placed that little calf in *shielding and prayers*. I hoped that the baby elephant could rejoin the herd, or at least it would find semblance and support in a sanctuary space.

Take, for example, the incredible work of IFS Officer Parveen Kaswan and his team, who successfully integrated an orphaned elephant into their department.

Robotic Elephants

Now, let's explore the robotic elephants, which are slowly picking up, and building an association with people/devotees because even a robotic elephant is a sight to behold.

Do we need to capture young ones and place them in institutions when there is no reference to it in any reliable doctrine? It appears that we are using cultural pretexts to justify unfair behaviour.

Sadly, it was happening at weddings in tourist destinations, like Goa. Thankfully the court has banned it.

Again, it comes down to the sheer exploitation and meaninglessness of our entertainment. Hence, why don't we embrace these 'reel' life robotic elephants and let the real ones be free, if not in the wild, at least in a sanctuary space, so that they live amidst their kind?

Let me use Elephant Naina to illustrate this. This beautiful soul was subjected to numerous relocations. Initially, she was employed in the logging industry, but when she injured her leg, she received no assistance. Instead, she was handed over to a religious institution, and finally into a begging elephant. Her impaired feet hindered her mobility, and she was in extreme distress. As her condition deteriorated, she was abandoned in an uncatered and dingy place.

Gratefully, animal advocates intervened and secured a good enough future for her, and she lived another 10 years. Although caregivers looked after her very well, her health had been severely compromised by years of mistreatment.

She was the first elephant with whom I formed a deep bond—a gentle and kind soul, even as her health steadily declined.

My initial encounter with these two lovely elephants caused me to break down. I came back and cried the entire evening and knew I wanted to do something for them. But to witness what she endured was heartbreaking. Nevertheless, her bond with a sanctuary elephant undoubtedly brought her much joy and unwavering support.

To really delve into, are we able to touch aspects of our Self, which need tending, which need care?

For me, that's what *Palakapya* Rishi signifies—to look inward! I am confident that it is within all of us. Just as we have the good and the bad; we have the ability for compassion.

Mainly, I wanted to bring this to ponder upon the impact we have on our surroundings and other beings. As Jane Goddall says, *"We are all influencing each other."* Perhaps a little more reflection will make us mindful!

Glamorising Captured and Captive Elephants

I want to address the capture of wild elephants, and the use of '*kumki*', a trained camp elephant used in operations to capture wild ones. The book 'Matriarch' vividly depicts this, showing how kumki elephants are trained to capture their own kind. While I understand there are exceptions, the kumkis are often over-glorified by the public. Would they do this of their own will?

The elephants, likewise in our state Karnataka, such as the Dasara elephants (Mysore Dasara—a festival where elephants are an integral part of the celebration) or those involved in captures, are made heroes.

Sadly, the wild elephant has been labelled a 'rogue' many a time.

The case in point especially is *Elephant Arjuna*—a lovely elephant. I had also met and interacted with him. It was an unfortunate death. Both the elephants were in *musth* (aggressive behaviours in bulls) and Arjuna, being over 60 years old, couldn't handle the younger elephant and he succumbed. This incident was sometime after Dussehra, where Arjuna was a major attraction with a mahout introducing him as Dhoni (India Cricketer).

However, even more distressing was the public making the wild elephant the culprit because Arjuna succumbed and demanded to capture and punish him akin to a criminal. During musth, bulls are prone to aggression and it's natural.

Do we need to glamorise captured and captive elephants and demonise the wild?

This trend is gaining momentum. There are social media and YouTube channels which glamorise these incidents. I wonder if any of these people have gone to a *Kraal* (a ground where captured wild elephants are initially kept) and or witnessed a capture. If one is in the right state of mind, it's hard not to perceive the loss of freedom and a natural life.

The Coorg and *Sakleshpur* belt in Karnataka has witnessed immense human-elephant negative interaction with enormous elephants being dislocated and placed in camps.

A distressing video depicted a mother and calf being captured in another location. Imagine the trauma on the young calf, especially.

Even at certain 'sites', elephants considered problematic or found roaming in human landscapes are captured. The situation remains complex.

If you look at the elephant's eyes, it will speak to you.

I vividly recall an elephant who had given birth recently, being very protective. Even as another calf came close, she kicked it away. I kept wondering what triggered this behaviour.

When I went back to the sanctuary and checked, our mahouts knew her and said, "Two of her calves had died earlier." Luckily, this calf pulled through, which explained her caution.

I also wonder about the emotional state of the wild elephants when they were born free, as they now see their young ones being restricted and having to move around in a small area. Since the mother is practically tied, the calf would be around her. The only solace was that the caretaker there was empathic. He used to call the Elephant baby '*Choti*,' and even informed them that he was going for a small lunch break. The response of the mother and calf was heartening.

When certain institutions cannot take care of all the elephants, they end up separating them. One mahout in particular told me how a calf was separated from the mother. She was still quite young, and he was quite heartbroken. Difficult to fathom how the elephants feel!

This facet is echoed in a touching *Malayalam*[7] poem, where the elephant was captured and became a temple elephant. It's festival time, and the ceremonies are going on. This writer beautifully captured what the elephant could be dreaming. Perhaps pining for the forest, the wild, the open skies, fresh grass and endless pathways. While the devotees may be engrossed in their devoted ritual, the elephant pining for its natural terrain. (Variath Kutty, 'Son of Sahya Ranges', 2013).

Imagine seeing the world through the eyes of an elephant. What could be the deepest longing?

"Kindness tames," stated Dr. A.J.T. John Singh, highlighting a co-centric approach towards elephants.

Certainly, we need more *Palakapyas* and *Shakuntalas*[8].

Shakuntala and *Dushyant*[9] are known for their love story. More significantly, she could communicate with animals, including the wild, a gift she passed on to her son 'Bharata,' who grew up in the forest. This approach is definitely the need of the hour.

Even personally, when one of our oldest elephants was sick, I started experiencing pain in the same area—my neck. During my trainings, I was told that this connection to all, including the source, elephants, and space, is a gift. However, it's important not to hold on to that energy because it can be overwhelming. I was advised to find a way to stay grounded and engage in the world.

Recently we had our AANE team meeting, and all of us were grateful to be of service, though sometimes it is emotionally challenging. I am often asked, "How do you handle it?" You absolutely must learn to disconnect and not internalise all that comes your way—it's incredibly difficult to witness the abuse.

For instance, I don't see elephants or any animal abuse videos with the sound on because one can break down. I also experienced rage and anger and had to learn how to channel it before it consumed me.

I started with welfare as it was the rehabilitation space that I was able to support, but then I gradually realised the number of captures that are happening because of our stupidity, overdrive and our insatiability. The lesser land, the more captures, the more problems and more negative interactions, eventually more captured and captive elephants. It's a vicious cycle. The only thing about camps is the elephants are with their own kind, but they're not entirely free.

Is that how they would have lived in the wild?

Animals are meant to move around and be in touch with the ground and nature. Be playful, be moving, and not like us. We have gone inactive, doesn't mean the animals will be the same. This explains why animals are experiencing a rise in health problems too.

The 'captive and capture' is a huge concern that needs to be looked into.

Hero Worship

The over glamorisation of heroism, I reckon, is there in the collective consciousness.

I work with cricketers and other elite athletes, and notice they are put on a pedestal. There is an expectation for heroes to be God-like and then they're brought down and demonised almost when they don't perform. Their families are attacked, and the hate is evident on social media.

Essentially, this is our own projection. Yes, one feels low, but then it's the expectation that we've placed. When it's not satisfied or unfulfilled, the anger spills out.

We need to reflect upon what is glamorous and what is dark in ourselves. How to hold these opposite polarities? We will touch a little more on these deeper, psychological insights, especially from a depth psychology perspective. As a collective, Thomas Singer, a Jungian writer, enquires, *"What needs birthing?"*

Today, as I write, marks *Aane Habba*[10], the birth of *Gajalakshmi*, a topic we'll explore in the final chapter. I think we need these festivities more; to revoke our ancient connection with the species and nature.

Ajay Desai, fondly called the 'Elephant Man of India,' urged that, *"We have a duty to protect them and be of service. Because they've served and aided humanity for 4000 years."* I would urge you to keep this in mind.

We need a greater number of individuals capable of empathising and displaying kindness towards the elephant's spirit, all while avoiding any physical proximity. Through this, elephants and humans can share the same space. Forest department and conservationists have been at the forefront of elephant preservation efforts, but it's a collective act.

Also, examining the role of media, which tends to heighten an issue, adds to people's perception and tolerance, especially of the current generation who are far removed from their roots.

Occasionally, we see videos that are heartening about co-existence. While we acknowledge that people are impacted, the real question is, how can we co-exist in this space? We have occupied their land, and with increasing human growth, it is vital to acknowledge our expansion in their territory.

A change in narrative, change in our thinking, "birthing of a new symbol," (Jung) is really needed. The Totem chapter will reflect more on this.

I am convinced elephants have a voice. They know how to converse. They trumpet, they vocalise, they rumble. If we tune in and invest the time and energy; if we sit with the discomfort, their discomfort and ours. Look into their eyes and listen. They're communicating all the time, perhaps not in words.

I think to be able to convey their message is my humble attempt. Precisely, why I do not believe in giving voice to the voiceless. Voiceless would be someone who's been utterly broken and dissociated. Despite that, they find their voice back as we see in safe, sanctuary places.

Let's not consider ourselves superior to this species, which is truly above us, and much more evolved.

Lantana Elephants

The Lantana elephants are made from the invasive lantana weed, which actually bring down the forest. What a brilliant concept to employ the locals and make these Elephants who have real-life counterparts bring out their message, and this travels across the world.

What a novel idea!

This is what makes our world better. These are the stories and inspirations that we need, the *Aane Mitras* (elephant friends), that the forest departments have tied up with locals who support, in conflict mitigation and early warning, because community support is paramount.

As urbanites, may we hold an empathy angle for everyone, including the communities, the elephants and nature.

May we listen to the elephant spirit, to our dreams, and let the symbol guide us before we lose the species.

Barbara Shor, in the 'Soul of the Wild,' believes *"They've come to evolve us."* Are we ready? Or are we going to bring them down, our own heritage species and Planet Earth? This is my thought at this juncture.

I sense things are shifting. We are evolving.

If you had asked me after my doctorate, even in my wildest dreams, I never would have imagined being so involved and interconnected with elephants. During my Jungian interview, something unexpected came up. The interviewer remarked, "It seems like you're the bridge between elephants and humans." I am humbled and will do my best.

May we all come together, and our energies rise to our highest self, imbibing the archetype or the energy of Palakapya. May we become the species we were always meant to be. Thus, as a collective, may we evolve.

I feel this would be *Palakapya's* message. May we tune into his energy, and of Gajalakshmi, so that we can always say 'Aane! Aane Banthu.'

People often ask me, "How do you bear witnessing this tragic space?" I usually respond, "It's the elephants who give us strength."

* * *

Reflections

1. Can we invoke the *Palakapya* in us?
2. How do we champion the elephant cause?
3. We're very proud and happy about our heritage. What about our culture have we imbibed?
4. How can we be more compassionate?

Notes

1. **Palakapya**: A sage credited with composing the *Hastaayurveda*, an ancient Sanskrit treatise on elephant care and health.
2. **Romapada**: A legendary King of Anga, who is associated with sage Palakapya and the cultural importance of elephants.
3. **The Matangalila**: A traditional text extolling the virtues and significance of elephants in Indian culture and spirituality.
4. **Hastaayurveda**: A classical work in Sanskrit focusing on veterinary practices and the well-being of elephants.
5. **Kingdom of Anga**: An ancient Indian region tied to the legend of Romapada and significant cultural narratives involving elephants.
6. **Messiahs**: Refers to saviours or protectors, in this context highlighting individuals or groups advocating for elephant conservation.
7. **Malayalam**: A Dravidian language predominantly spoken in Kerala, a region culturally linked with elephants through festivals and traditions.
8. **Shakuntala**: The central character in Kalidasa's *Abhijnanasakuntalam*, symbolising harmony with nature and animals.
9. **Dushyant**: A king and consort of Shakuntala, featured in tales that often intertwine with nature and conservation themes.
10. **Aane Habba**: An elephant festival in South India, notably in Karnataka, celebrating elephants' cultural and religious importance.

SECTION 2
PSYCHE, SOUL, AND SYMBOLISM

Chapter 4

DREAM SIGNIFICANCE AND BEFRIENDING THE OTHER

"Befriending the Other."
Who really is 'the other'? Is it them, or a hidden part of our own Self?
Like the faces in dreams, mere reflections of who we are,
different, yet the same.
When we approach 'the other' with the eyes of a child,
curious and playful, full of wonder —
We open our minds and soften our hearts.
Defences fall away, and we glimpse the similarities beneath the surface.
As curiosity blossoms, so does our connection.
We begin to care, to feel passion.
Until one day, it transforms into love.
When we love, we wish to protect, to preserve.
Perhaps this is the message the elephants offer —
a call to safeguard what we cherish.
And my invitation. —CS.

As we venture into one of my favourite topics—*dreams*—the above passage beautifully invokes the spirit of the elephant. It urges us to consider the value of befriending and understanding 'the other,' both within ourselves and the environment. I hope this sparks inspiration in you and encourages you to inspire others, creating a ripple effect. Let us be guided by the depths of our psychic world, as emphasised by visionary thinkers such as *Sri Ramanuja*[1].

In this exploration of dreams, we will primarily focus on elephant dreams. So, get ready to dive into this adventure with the sacred elephants that grace our lives, bringing their divine blessings.

Dream Tradition

In India, we have heard of the tradition of the Goddess appearing in the dreams of inspirers, such as *Kalidasa*[2], *Tenali Rama*[3] *and Ramanuja*.

For *Sri Ramanuja*, "an equation had no meaning unless it revealed the mind of God". To him, "the mind of God is the Goddess". As per records, the Goddess revealed the equations to him in dreams. We could say he was in touch with the inner realm through the divine feminine, which we will explore in the last segment of the book.

Lord *Vishnu*[4], creating the world through his dream, explains the importance given to the dreamscape in Hinduism especially.

My attempt is to get you to connect to your dreams, which is also inner nature, as Jung and many other schools assert. *Sri Aurobindo*[5] talks of integral yoga and the impact of dreams. Buddhism and *Sufism*[6] also give importance. In fact, one particular sect stands out in my memory from our guide in Istanbul, Turkey. He shared the story of a teacher who, even after his passing, continued to guide his students through dreams. This is the incredible power of our inner dream world.

Naturally, the initial question that may arise is, 'Oh, but I can't recall my dreams, or my dreams are incredibly strange and nonsensical.' And I'll be honest, sometimes even I wake up and think, 'What was that dream about? It was so weird.'

Jungian Depth Psychology integrates dream work, and that's how I speak with conviction from working and enhancing my life through dream guidance.

Let's start by delving into one of the most significant dreams in history, which was documented thousands of years ago—the dream of *Buddha's*[7] birth.

The legend goes that Queen *Mahamaya*, Buddha's mother, before conceiving him, had a dream where she's taken away to a sacred place, bathed in a holy river, made to lie down, anointed with sacred herbs/perfumes and prepared for a sacred ritual. Then a divine white elephant circles her three times, offers a white lotus, and finally enters her womb from the right side. She wakes up hearing the peacock's call, and the dream is interpreted as an important and auspicious one, predicting the child would be a great leader, either a king or monk. We can see this depiction in quite a few temples, especially of Buddhist origin.

It's fascinating to see this emblem of an elephant entering the Queen's womb. In fact, I got to know this while preparing for an Elephant symbolism talk, given to a Jungian group. I had only known the elephants for a year, yet they fascinated me, and I researched all the things connected to elephants. Over time, I began to realise how rich their history is, and how they've supported and helped mankind throughout the ages. Isn't that amazing?

And why, you may wonder, is this dream so significant to me? There's a remarkable quote by Buddha himself that highlights the immense significance of elephants in Buddhism: "Among all footprints, that of the elephant is supreme."

Furthermore, Buddhists hold the belief that if Buddha were to be reborn, it would be in his favourite form of an elephant. This magnificent creature is seen as a representation of Buddha himself, symbolising profound significance. I came across another intriguing legend recently, which suggests that the elephant is actually Buddha's elder brother.

Befriending the Other

"We cherish and protect what we love. Curiosity with respect may enlarge our perspective about the other/unknown species and beings."

Whilst exploring the emblem, let us look into the aspect of befriending. You may wonder about the purpose of 'befriending the other' and who specifically is being referred to as the 'other'.

This is crucial because what we perceive as 'the other' or 'the unknown' often intimidates us. If something scares us, we often try to confront, overpower, or conquer it. When we look at the 'other' with the curiosity or wonder of a child, it embodies pure innocence. We focus on being open to possibilities rather than adopting a fearful and defensive mindset. Of course, it is wise to maintain a safe distance from elephants, whether in the wild or in captivity and not foolishly venture too close physically.

Sometimes, I notice my dogs become fascinated by an ant or a fly. What's intriguing is that it can be the same ant that continues to attract them. I believe it's because they are 'present in the moment', finding joy in the little things.

This got me thinking about the concept of 'befriending' and how it can enhance our lives. If we approach life with curiosity and wonder, we can play with new ideas and thoughts that spark our interest. Gradually, this interest can turn into a passion that drives us. We may even find ourselves falling in love with something, as we genuinely desire to engage and make it a part of our lives.

It's essential to understand that if we don't like or care about something, we are not going to invest our energy. So, where do we choose to invest our energy? Typically, we prioritise and focus on things that inspire and move us. I recently discovered this interesting concept: if you have an idea, don't let it go, give it energy and honestly, what we give our energy to—grows.

A prime example of this is the *Chipko movement*[8], which illustrates how the tree huggers loved and wished to protect the trees. They were not merely fighting against the system or the people who wanted to cut down the trees.

I will always cherish the memory of my first psychology lesson, taught to me by my beloved Ajji (grandmother). She instilled in me the understanding of how focusing and building the right energy can lead us to what we truly want. She did this through the concept of *tathastu* (blessing). Each time there was a scarcity of rice, for example at home, my Ajji would say, "*akki hechide*" (there is surplus rice).

This confused me as a young child, especially when I overheard my Ajja (grandfather) saying that he still hadn't bought rice. I asked why we needed more rice when there was already a surplus. It was then that my grandmother sat me down and explained the importance of being mindful of our speech and thoughts, as the asthu devatas (God of Blessings) may say tathastu anytime.

In a heartfelt conversation, she explained the fascinating tale of the asthu devatas, divine beings known as the gods of blessings, who possess the incredible ability to bestow their blessings upon us at any given time. If we are not mindful, we will continue to attract what we do not desire. I later discovered that it is a fundamental principle in psychology. Even to this day, this practice continues to be followed within our home.

For example, when an athlete recouping from injury is rehabilitating, we gradually shift their focus on returning to play (RTP) and performance so that the mind shifts its focus to the present and future goals, and not merely obsesses over the past and re-injury.

Also, coming back to dreams, they not only capture our attention, but they also help us address our one-sided perspectives. They offer hope and healing through supportive symbols during difficult times. Nightmares, on the other hand, serve as a wake-up call when we ignore their messages. Repetitive dreams signify important transitions that we must pay attention to. We will explore these types of dreams in more detail later.

Ever since I was young, I have had a deep personal connection with elephants. The songs *Aane Bantu Aane* and *Gajanana* have been ingrained in my psyche since I was a child. I would often sing these songs to my young niece, and it was interesting to see that she also had a strong empathy for elephants. Her understanding encompasses both captivity and freedom. Rather than being kept alone and subjected to abuse in private institutions solely for our entertainment, she longs to see the elephants in the forests roaming freely with their herd.

The compassion shared among the young is uplifting to observe. The foundation of empathy begins at home with our attitudes. Children are the future generation, and that's why our group, AANE—'All About the Nature of Elephants', strives to create awareness and build youth teams who can blossom into fervent champions of elephant welfare and conservation.

A forest officer observed that some people find it simpler to view elephants in zoos than on safaris in parks or forests. But we need to question our actions. During a trip to Wayanad in Kerala, we passed through a national park. At first, I was excited about seeing elephants, but when I noticed a mother and a young calf, I immediately wished for them to stay in the protected forest area to avoid any potential harm from passing vehicles on the roads.

It's important to consider how the species must feel when we invade their home for our convenience. We are looking at psychological safety as much as physical safety.

Can we look at this issue with compassion and embrace all beings? We will explore this further in the next section.

Dream Work

Another aspect to consider is the depth psychology perspective, which focuses on integrating the otherness or our shadow. For instance, we can look at others in our dreams, as they may represent aspects that require our attention. Through 'others,' we may become aware of traits that we have not acknowledged in ourselves, both positive and negative, which are often projected onto external circumstances. By reclaiming these projections, we can avoid conflict and promote the development of individuals and society, ultimately leading to the resolution of many issues in the world.

"Dreams are true and given by God."—Sri Ramanuja (Sri Bashyam).

Now you must be thinking, "What are my dreams?" Before I begin, I want to ask if you've had a dream about an elephant or the deity Ganesha we earlier discussed. If the answer is yes, when exactly? I mean, at what juncture in your life did this dream occur? Did it signify something to you? Did it make sense to you? What meaning did you make of what was happening in your conscious life, or so-called daily life, or waking life, because dreams always connect to our life?

I found Jung's statement that dreams are *teleological* to be intriguing. In his view, life is teleological—that there is meaning to life.

Let me start by highlighting that my strong bond with nature in Malnad has greatly influenced and shaped my experiences with elephants. I've always had a deep fondness for these majestic creatures.

As I began my Jungian training and analysis, I started dreaming a lot more about elephants. Initially, it was exciting, especially with baby elephants. Gradually, I came to realise that there's a lot more here. Besides, we hold the belief that each animal symbolises something. What was the meaning and message of the mighty giants to me?

It's interesting to note that the meaning of a dream can vary depending on one's personal experiences and feelings towards a particular animal. For example, a dog lover might interpret a dream involving a dog differently than someone who is afraid of dogs or who is unconnected to a specific animal.

With this in mind, I decided to examine my dreams of elephants more closely. I started wondering why they appeared so frequently in my dreams. This led me to contemplate it, as *Deepak Chopra*[10] ponders if we are being dreamt. So, *were the elephants dreaming me?*

Jung believed the elephant serves as a symbol of the Self, a topic that we will delve into in subsequent chapters.

Over time, a noticeable theme began to take shape. Just before the elephants came into my waking life in 2019 after my birthday as a gift, I found myself dreaming of them more frequently. The experience of meeting these magnificent creatures is indescribable; it possessed an otherworldly, almost dreamlike quality as if my dreams were priming me for this encounter. Even though I had witnessed wild elephants and met them in different camps before, nothing could have prepared me for this surreal experience.

The deep connect with one of the sweetest elephants I have come across ripped open my soul. It saddens me to witness the harm we, as humans, have inflicted upon this beautiful soul. Despite enduring physical and mental abuse, she displayed remarkable gentleness and grace, qualities that will forever stay with me.

In my dreams, elephants filled my being, both before and after the encounter. They seemed to signal something important. The thrill of meeting them was beyond words, but curiously enough, I began to have a repetitive dream that I feel compelled to share.

"I dream that I am communing with an elephant. It's the matriarch and we are in deep conversation or communion."

I would wake up in awe and feel held, but I would not remember what the elephant was communicating to me. I knew it was important, but for the life of me, I couldn't remember what it was, and this dream kept repeating.

It's best not to force meaning or analyse it too much. Just let it be and wait for the meaning to come naturally. Interact with the dream, sit with it, and engage with it. Also, be cautious of scary internet interpretations that might frighten you. The dream speaks directly to the dreamer, but the themes can be universal and archetypal.

Now, if I've piqued your interest. Yes, I comprehended the 'symbolism' in the recurring dreams. If I hadn't done it, this book you're reading wouldn't exist. Perhaps you'd want to see if you got an inkling before reading ahead.

It was only after I accepted my deep connection, and that I could play a role in elephant well-being, did the repetitive dream stopped. I was in a way in awe, but there was more to it. The matriarch—the elephant spirit was communicating the message to me, which took a while to digest and accept since I am a part of the over-rationalised society too!

Dream Tending

I began to notice the impact of my presence on the elephants, our relationship and that they felt safe with me, I could calm them, too. My psychology training perhaps played a significant role over here. I rejoiced that they liked me, cared for and protected me, too. I was humbled to be accepted by the small herd. It took some time, but eventually, I awakened and knew with unwavering certainty that this was also my path, my calling. Then, just like that, the pivotal dream stopped after heading for the message.

Surely, the matriarch was signalling me to wake up and wholly accept my destiny or calling, whatever one chooses to call it. She must have thought, "Ah, finally you get it."

Prior to the elephants becoming a part of my life, there was another dream. Perhaps, I could say at least 8–10 years earlier. This dream has always stayed with me, as it carried a powerful numinous (divine) energy. Back then, I lacked the knowledge of working with dreams, so I couldn't fully understand it, even though I sensed it was a significant dream, known as a 'big dream' in Jungian terms. The dream unfolds this way:

"I am in a vast open natural space and a little girl, Caucasian girl, is walking with an elephant, and stands right in front of me. She is holding the elephant trunk, and we are all silently communicating. As we gaze at one another, a silent understanding passes between us effortlessly. Then, sitting on the elephant, the girl suddenly flies away, and as they flew/soar upward like a bird, the elephant and the girl become one."

The dream was awe-inspiring, and my admiration for it remains. I recall being informed by a known person with a spiritual inclination that it could be the Earth Goddess, *Bhoomi Devi*. She definitely possessed that radiant, celestial aura. One might consider if it was predicting my future journey well in advance. I wondered, was I truly that little girl who formed an unbreakable bond with the magnificent elephant? It is a thought worth contemplating even now.

At the time of my dream, I had just come back from Australia after finishing my PhD. Even in my wildest dreams, I wouldn't have thought of our paths intertwining and becoming so pivotal in my life. Being accepted by the elephant herd and the elephant community has been very humbling, and I am aware I am just touching the tip of the iceberg and have a long way to go akin to this dream. Echoing Robert Frost, *"I still have miles to go before I sleep…"*

I wonder what my bond is with these beings. Not everyone who dreams of a particular animal might get involved with that species. Little did I know that our lives were going to get entwined. Importantly, what they evoked in me was an 'invitation and initiation to the depths'. I had to touch my vulnerability and work on certain aspects which then helped in connecting me to them, to my core inner self and the feminine in an overly masculine world.

Elephantine Energy

During a critical juncture in my sports psychology journey, I found myself collaborating with a renowned high-profile team. While explaining emergence during a team session, I drew parallels between my work with elephants and its relevance to the field. Synchronously, I was standing in the centre of the team, and it was, again, an all-male team.

On the screen was the treasured photo of me with elephants, the two earliest beautiful elephants who embraced me and guided me ever so gently. The team reflected an impression of awe and respect. It was at that moment that I sensed a genuine acceptance from the team. It was as if they were thinking, "If she can handle elephants, she can handle anything!"

Incidentally, we were in a circle, and I was standing in the centre, and it felt whole and complete. That also marked the beginning of the shift of my equation with them. Prior to this, I had the dream of an elephant herd visiting me, assuring me onward. Then the emergence theme with elephants in the background absolutely had their energy not just around me but also the team.

"*Whenever we touch nature, we get clean. People who have gotten dirty through too much civilisation take a walk in the woods, or a bath in the sea, allowing nature to touch them. It can be done within or without. Walking in the woods, lying on the grass, taking a bath are from the outside; entering the unconscious through dreams is touching nature from the inside, things are set right again."*—Carl Jung (Dream Analysis, p.142).

I am inviting you to contemplate your own dreams. Look at what your dreams are and amplify them because they are important. It's really one of nature. It can take us to our deeper selves, helping us realise where we are stuck and perhaps showing what is to come in life. Of course, we also have precognitive dreams. For example, there are times when I kind of know that a specific elephant is a little agitated, or there's something amiss in the space (place) through dreams. Have you begun reflecting on what your dreams might be telling you? What do you understand from this section?

Why is it so important, and what happens to us when we are not dreaming, or when we are having a particular dream or theme? For instance, this young athlete of mine would frequently dream of being chased by a wild animal. She was terrified and would wake up in fear and panic. This elite athlete, in fact, was going through a lot at that point in time and was also facing intense anxiety. The dreams were clearly telling her that there was something she was not looking at. I had to steadily provide the holding, the safe container and build her up (ego strength) and eventually get her to face the animal.

What was she running from? Why was she running from it? What would be the way forward? Did the animal have a message and was trying to get her attention? This is a common dream for most of us. But we're too scared that we want to run away in our dreams. We're petrified in real life also that we may want to escape or try to overpower it, so it will not harm us! We see this happening across the world, and this is to understand why 'befriending the other' is very imperative.

Remember 'the blind men and elephant' story, where each gives a varied response based on their perception. Can we be open to different views? What is the other trying to communicate, becomes the central concern. What does the elephant mean to you? Is it only about Lord Ganesha, the elephant-headed God?

Wonder what Ganesha would say when he sees the Self, the elephant in captivity, being abused. The divine in the elephant symbol has lost its energy, its power because it has been concretised and abused. The question to inquire is what we are holding captive in ourselves, and what can we do?

Let us ask ourselves which inner animal or instinct is awaiting to be reborn, to rewild, to recalibrate? Can we live harmoniously with the elephants, with these mighty beings, the gentle giants, and give them their rightful place—free and wild in their own habitat though it's shrinking?

Symbols in Dreams

What is the new symbol that we need to birth as a culture? Hopefully, our dreams will guide us in our endeavour. First, we need to begin by engaging with the collective shadow of our society, so that it may spark a transformation in attitude and mindset.

Whilst preparing for the Elephant symbolism talk, the symbol guided me, and it has become a living symbol since then. The trunk held me in many dreams akin to the elephants in real life. What I mean is that the elephant trunk has the power to hold me through the elephant's spirit or energy if it resonates better. More on this in the Totem chapter.

Let me close this chapter by sharing this beautiful dream, which brought solace while I grappled with the heartbreaking loss of our first and beloved elephant. This loss was a tragic outcome of the harmful effects of human actions on her well-being. As she was making her final transition and I was struggling to cope, this dream held us all at the sanctuary.

"As I am watching the ritual performed on our dear elephant, she awakens and becomes a beautiful young goddess, looking straight into my eyes."

Even as she transitioned, she made sure to provide a comforting dream that I revisited frequently, as we grieved her physical loss. Knowing she's with us in spirit is comforting.

I hope you're getting a glimpse of the healing power of dreams. No wonder there are dream temples dedicated specifically for the healing purpose.

On the occasion of *Shivratri*[11], I came back upset as I couldn't visit the temple due to the looming crowd. Adding to the conversation, my mother insisted that we should have waited and not left the temple without seeking blessings. I felt dejected and fell asleep that night with thoughts of my beloved *Ishta* (favourite)—Lord Shiva, and to my surprise, I had a dream where I was blessed with his divine *darshan*[12] (grace) and woke up filled with joy.

"I dream of a huge Shiva statue amidst a natural water body akin to an ocean."

The question I and perhaps what the elephants are asking is to awaken our own soul, to reconnect to ourselves, and the world soul. I am going to leave you with this thought.

May the elephants guide you in your dreams, in your reverie, in your fantasy, and see what this symbolises. When you honour and embrace your dreams, the more you will dream.

I end the chapter with this lovely dream: "the four baby elephant figurines literally came to life as I am looking at them."

I hope to establish a fresh approach to bond with and show deep respect for these exquisite beings, rooted in an understanding of their authentic nature, guided by our dreams and the sacred elephants.

* * *

Reflections

1. What's emerging in your inner space right now?
2. Any dreams coming up from memory?
3. Pay attention to your dreams by setting an intent and dream book.
4. Honour the dream with a little seed sowing.

Notes

1. **Sri Ramanuja:** 11th-century Hindu theologian known for the non-dualism philosophy.

2. **Kalidasa**: Renowned classical Sanskrit poet and dramatist, author of Shakuntala and Meghaduta.
3. **Tenali Rama**: 16th-century poet and court jester famous for his wit in court.
4. **Vishnu**: Hindu deity, the preserver of the universe, known for his avatars like Rama and Krishna.
5. **Sri Aurobindo**: Indian philosopher and yogi known for his Integral Yoga and teachings on spiritual evolution.
6. **Sufism**: A mystical branch of Islam focusing on divine love and inner purification through meditation and poetry.
7. **Buddha**: Refers to Siddhartha Gautama, the founder of Buddhism.
8. **Chipko Movement**: 1970s Indian environmental movement where villagers hugged trees to prevent deforestation.
9. **Teleological**: Concept that entities have an inherent purpose or goal (telos), used in psychology to denote meaning-driven processes.
10. **Deepak Chopra**: Indian American author and advocate of alternative medicine, combining Eastern spirituality with Western science.
11. **Shivratri**: Hindu festival dedicated to Lord Shiva, celebrated with fasting and night-long worship.
12. **Darshan**: The auspicious sight of a deity or revered person considered a spiritual blessing.

"To say no to rides is to make space for their yes—to roam, to live, to be."

Chapter 5

MY LITTLE ONE ~ LEELA AND OUR JOURNEY

Vision:

As I drummed and entered the lush green forest,
I had the vision of 'Leela', who greeted in her customary manner,
She led me to a large herd by the riverbanks,
with whom I felt an ancient connect,
like they were my family.
They welcomed me like I am one amongst them.
It seemed like they were awaiting me.
This vision repeated on many occasions,
after Leela came into my life.—CS.

As I began writing this chapter, I was teary-eyed; she tugs my very soul and this beautiful little ring that I wear, where the elephant trunk entwines my finger, talks of our connection.

A year before the elephants came into my life, I had taken to *shamanism*[1] and gifted myself a beautiful drum. I remember when I would drum and intend to journey (go) to my power place. I started to sense their footsteps, the rumbles, the trumpeting of elephants, and lots of elephants. This happened in my office space, which is also my inner sanctum. I opened my eyes to see if they were actually present. Intensely strong was the journey, as they call it, in shamanism.

On another occasion, while drumming for a friend, a similar occurrence took place. It was then that I began comprehending the extraordinary and profound connection I shared with elephants. I pondered whether they were my spirit animals and if I belonged to the elephant tribe. Many have remarked that I possess an elephant's soul.

Now, let me introduce you to my little one, Leela, and the way we greet each other. It starts with me calling out her name, "Leela!" … "rumbling sounds (low)", then a little peeking. "Leela!" … "Ah, it's really her!" … "rumbling sounds"—deep rumbling… and she moves towards me…

Imagine this enormous elephant, standing at eight feet tall and weighing around 10,000 pounds, almost jogging just to reach me faster. The mahout would say, "*hallu, hallu*", meaning, 'wait, wait, slow down', but she's determined to run towards me. Once she is with me, she greets by touching and caressing with her trunk. Now and then, she even urinates out of excitement, which is a common behaviour among animals.

Then begins the trunk talk along with constant vocalising and rumbling and we commune. This goes on for a few minutes until she senses, feels, and holds me. I whisper into her trunk, caress it, and hug her with my small arms. Occasionally, she touches my forehead with her own, creating a special connection between us. She expresses she misses me. This is what I sense.

This is how Leela welcomes me every single instance we meet. She is exuberant with joy as she sees me and so am I. Just picturing this and our bond gladdens me, despite being far away from her.

I invite you to take a moment to imagine this scene and see what emotional response it evokes. Switch off your rational mind and simply picture this connection between a young adult elephant (female) and a human being. Though I am quite small, she leans down so we can touch our foreheads, and I feel at par with her. In this precious space, nothing and no one else matters to either of us.

How did this little one take to me? You must wonder, and so do I. I doubt I will ever find the answer, but that's alright. It's the beauty of life—some mysteries are meant to be lived rather than solved.

This little one is the same elephant who welcomes me when I drum and visit the power place. In the metaphysical realm, she is my spirit guide, and in the physical realm, she is my little companion. She is my living goddess, guiding me through life, even though she sometimes whines, and I chide or pamper her akin to a mother.

Leela loves to play with me and can be mischievous when she's a little annoyed or when I am not giving her attention, especially if I am focusing on another elephant. When I am eating and she's in a separate enclosed space or shed, she covers herself in mud, and looks like a *'manina gombe'* (mud doll)—an endearing sight! I am poured a trunkful of mud and everyone else delights, including the mahouts. I, on the other hand, prefer to avoid the mud bath because of my sensitive skin and hair, but I don't mind, though I chid her for it in a light-hearted way. Occasionally, I try to run away from her, and she playfully chases after me. I suggest to "Shake off all the mud," and as she runs, it shakes off her body. I then remark, "You know, I don't enjoy being sprinkled with so much mud." It falls on deaf ears as usual!

This is my little one, Leela, whom I first met in 2020, a year after I had met and bonded with our other two dear elephants—my initiators into the elephant world. Our first encounter surprises me to date, like many other things about us, that has me amazed. Just like it has others.

The First Meeting

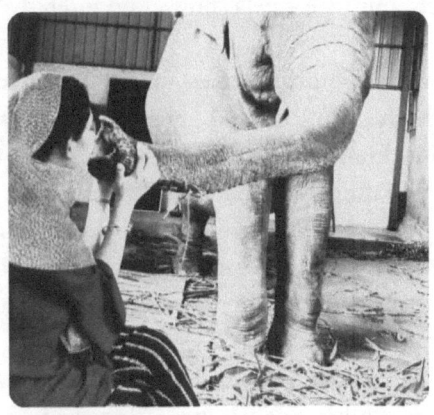

We stepped into a shed-like space, and gently asked, "Oh, is your name, Leela," and she responded "ooohhh" with the vocalisation that we see with captive elephants. I am amazed by her response because I had not encountered an elephant that would vocalise in such a human-like manner.

I don't know what she sensed, what she felt, or is it an ancient bond between us? Is it possible that we have known each other before? Do I have an elephant soul, or are we part of the same soul tribe?

If you are spiritually inclined and familiar with these concepts, you may want to contemplate them. Even if you experience resistance, it's alright. This was exactly my sentiment then, and it remains so. Surprisingly, she continued to vocalise through our time together…

Her earlier mahout, the one she had at the older institution, at first advised me to be careful because she doesn't take to strangers easily. Indeed, she's not particularly fond of humans, mainly those she doesn't know. Of course, I maintained a safe distance and was cautious. Also, I was recovering from a foot fracture, and my balance was still a little shaky.

It was remarkable that this beautiful, yet massive elephant in the prime of her life started to show interest in communing, talking, and playing with me. The mahout was equally shocked and surprised as I was, and eventually, he relaxed. A good friend accompanied me, but despite her efforts, our little Leela showed no interest. She even ignored the mahout.

When I was attempting to establish a connection with Leela through the mahout, I noticed that her vocalisation started increasing. She began getting louder and louder. The mahout interpreted, "She wants to talk to you more." We had brought jackfruit, which elephants absolutely love, and he was feeding it to her. As a result, her trunk became slightly sticky, but she started offering it to me. Elephants use their trunks to communicate with those they have a bond with, including humans.

Perhaps she desired companionship and sought it with me because my interest in her was sincere, rather than wanting a photo or entertainment.

However, I was naturally hesitant, since this was my first meeting with a totally new elephant. I positioned myself a little distance away from her, knowing that an elephant's trunk can cause significant harm if swung at you, regardless of it being just a gesture to tell you to move away. But she persistently extended her trunk to me, and eventually, I cautiously held it and spoke through it. She seemed to want me to repeat the gesture, and this continued throughout our entire meeting. I witnessed her being an elephant and curiously engaged with her. It seems to have struck a chord in the young one who sought authentic connection and was not objectified for entertainment.

My friend in the space didn't seem to matter to Leela. She didn't respond to her mahout, nor did he interfere. She wanted me to talk to no one but her. I stayed with her for about two hours, and it seemed as if we had always known each other.

At one point I said, "Oh, I have hurt my leg here (pointing), and it is still healing." Surprisingly, she brought her trunk and gently touched the exact spot where I was hurt (the metatarsal). My friend and I were astonished. We thought she couldn't have understood, but then she continued to bring her trunk to the exact location. It was as if she was trying to heal or soothe the injured area.

I think that moment, that day of connection, was intensely beautiful. Similar to when I met our other two elephants for the first time, especially our dear sweet elephant, whom we recently lost.

It was magically enchanting. We spent two hours there, and I felt that something within me, my body, mind and soul, completely opened up. I returned soulfully joyous. Thus, the journey with this little one began.

The Unlikely Elephant Shelter/Shed

Earlier, she used to belong to an institution and was kept in a cramped-up place that was unsuitable for an elephant. Unfortunately, it was in an industrial area. Whilst searching for the location to meet her, I asked our veterinarian, "Are you sure this is the place?" Leela was in a shed, isolated from the natural habitat, and living with the mahout's family, along with dogs and even hens. She was tied up both in the front and back on hard concrete, which is detrimental to an elephant's legs and can cause long-term problems.

The distressing reality of elephants living among humans is disheartening. Many captive elephants, in particular, suffer from severe foot and arthritic issues due to standing for long hours on harsh ground while being tethered. What's worse is that they remain tied up in the same spot where they defecate. They furthermore end up with severe joint and knee issues, compromising their well-being. Their toes, feet and padding are meant for walking on mud and being in the wild, not for walking and standing on hard concrete.

Fortunately, Leela's legs are fine, although she did have some minor issues. It was distressing to see a young elephant full of energy confined in such a small area. The question that arises is, what purpose do they serve among us?

Leela's previous location is quite far on the outskirts of Bengaluru, but I started visiting her by contacting the mahout and spent a few hours with her. During my second visit, it seemed as if there had been no gap at all. She welcomed me as if I were an old friend. She wanted my attention, and even the mahout started to ease with my presence. I began feeding her with fruits and holding her trunk when she offered. Of course, the mahout was invariably there. I must have visited her around 4–5 times. At last, we were able to free her from that place.

Transitions and Shifting

When we transferred her to the rehabilitation centre, what occurred was that the previous mahout didn't stay long. When I went and saw her the next day, it was a picture of deep pain because she was in utter distress. It seems the old mahout tied her there and left because of some personal issues, thinking we could manage, suggesting, "Chaitanya Madam knows her." At first, I thought he was joking because while I could interact with elephants in their presence, I hadn't imagined taking care of one by myself, as I am not a trained mahout. I didn't think I would be able to "unchain her" in mahout terms.

As soon as I entered, her stress was evident. It's understandable, considering she was in an unfamiliar place with no one she knew. As I approached her, one of our mahouts said, "Oh, be careful. This elephant is very stressed and not in a good state." I assured them, "I know this elephant," and from a distance where she could see me, I called out, "Leela". Instantly, she responded with a familiar rumble and turned towards me. It was clear that she was relieved to hear a calm and familiar voice.

Then, she noticed me and we made eye contact. She began vocalising and reached out with her trunk. The surrounding staff was surprised and tensed, so I also moved carefully. This was uncharted territory for me, a new space, because her known mahout was not present, and it was my first time seeing her so stressed. Thankfully, she began to calm down in my presence. I kept calling her name very softly to reassure her and continued stroking her trunk when she reached out. As she became calmer, I started to feed fodder and fruits from a distance. The atmosphere around us began to relax as well.

It was noteworthy that she treated me with tenderness, while exhibiting angst towards others, especially the mahouts, because of fear and anxiety. When approached at first, she threw stones, mud or anything she could find at others. It was a difficult period for everyone involved.

I visited her every day until she became more settled, gradually reducing my visits since the new place was quite a distance. The time and effort I had invested in building a relationship with her resulted in trusting me. And even now, it's heartwarming.

In fact, I had planned to go on a trip and consulted one of our veterinarians about it. She shook her head in disapproval, and I decided to cancel the trip because I knew that this little one needed me at the time. Even if I had travelled, my mind would have been preoccupied with thoughts of her and how she was doing. So, it took a while for things to normalise. This was a critical period of change for her, much like a rebirth, and it was not easy for her, either.

During this period, I was also supporting my close cousin brother, who was suffering from a terminal illness and was in critical condition. While there was a physical death on one end, there was a rebirth for the young elephant on the other. Even to this day, the mahouts express their highest praise of 'unchaining her'.

Initially, when the mahouts would leave us alone at a distance, I wasn't sure that I could read and understand her fully. However, whether it was the old mahout or the new ones, they all knew that she trusted and relied on me. She would follow me sweetly, without any command.

At times, when the mahouts had tasks to attend to, they would leave me in charge and offer the stick. But I always declined, saying, "No, I don't need that." Although now I carry a stick due to my recent knee surgery, to ensure stability on the uneven ground. I make it clear by telling Leela, "The stick is not meant for you, but for me to walk with." I never want her to feel that it's for her. She understands this, and I am grateful for it!

Let's pause for a moment. I want you to see what's coming up for you.

Are you in disbelief? Are you filled with awe?

The Healing Journey Begins

Remember the movie 'My Octopus Teacher'? If you haven't watched it yet, I highly recommend you do. It explores a heartwarming relationship between a diver and an octopus. They become good friends, and the movie showcases their bond and how the octopus would eagerly await the diver's arrival. The diver documents their journey over 365 days, capturing their mutual care and concern. Sadly, the octopus passes away, as it is known that they die after giving birth. The diver reflects on the incredible journey they shared and emphasises the importance of being more in sync with nature. Take a moment to reflect on your own encounters in the natural world.

This also brings to mind a feral cat that found its way into our house. He was a young kitten and slowly won me over. My family has historically had a phobia with cats, and while I had learned to endure them, this particular one opened me up. It even gave me a gentle love bite before one day disappearing. Over time, its visits became less frequent. At home, there were different opinions, such as "Oh, it must have found a different route." But I couldn't help but think if there was more to it. Because, even when satiated, it would keep calling, it would want to play a little. I did sense a strong connection.

I sometimes wondered, "Could it be?" Then, we saw an older cat that used to intimidate the young one. It made me realise that there could be other factors at play, like fear and avoidance. However, our bond remains strong. Hopefully, as the young cat grows stronger, it may return to visit us.

We can never fully know what is on their (animals) minds. However, their actions, love, and trust speak volumes.

I believe there are many other aspects to consider, and that's something we should keep in mind. I am hoping that wherever it is, he's fine. Perhaps it will return at some point unless it has already come for a specific reason. Cats are known to ward off negative energy, so that's a possibility.

It was the time I was beginning to write and was getting okay with showing more of myself and being seen a lot more in the world. So, did the cat come due to that reason?

A key aspect I learned from the animal communication course is that animals come into our lives at certain times. I've known this to some extent, but it reaffirmed my belief and showed how they mirror us. They take on a lot of our issues. Also, they could really be mirroring what we need to work on, or at times even take on health issues. There's a connect from beyond.

I brought this up because I too wonder about these aspects and my connection with Leela. At times, you meet someone and instantly feel a kinship. I have mentioned this to some students and said, "You look very familiar. I probably know you from somewhere."

As I mentioned earlier, both Leela and I took to each other from the outset. How did this so-called aggressive elephant in human terms, who doesn't take much to anyone else, including to some members of the old mahout's family, took to me from the word go? Our relationship has only grown stronger. Certainly, there have been instances, although rare, when she has been a little distant due to something she's dealing with and it's best to give her space.

At times, akin to other elephant handlers, I got hurt by their tail, feet, or when they moved their trunk, and I was in the wrong place. This happened to Leela once, when she was drowsy. She moved her trunk just as I was nearby. I swiftly moved my hands and accidentally touched the stone pillar next to me, causing me to exclaim, "Oh!" in pain.

As soon as she realised that I had been hurt, she appeared apologetic and repeatedly checked to make sure I was okay. It was nothing major, but I believe it rewired something in her because she has been cautious around me ever since. Especially during my recovery from a knee injury, when my balance was unsteady. I remember one particular incident when I was still using a crutch and accidentally became a little off-balance while stepping over a piece of bark. I reacted on my instinct and said, "Ah." Both the mahout and Leela panicked, thinking I might fall. Leela let out a loud scream. The mahout swiftly held me and helped me regain my balance, but it took a moment to assure her that I was fine, repeatedly saying, "I am okay, I am okay." It was as if she was showing the kind of concern one would have for a loved one.

This kind of incident has happened on numerous occasions. She frequently detects my distress and pain, even as I stumble or accidentally hit myself due to my oversight. For instance, when I fail to notice pillars or barricades ahead of me while standing in the sun.

Akin to Leela, most elephants are deeply affected when their herd experiences pain or distress. In fact, she appears to have an intuition for sensing my own troubles, like the time when the car tyre burst on the highway while returning home. I witnessed both her and the other elephants raising their trunks as if blessing me before I left the sanctuary, akin to encircling me in a safe space. I honestly think their shielding protected us and prevented any harm. The driver promptly detected the car issue and stopped. The road was a highway, fortunately, with few vehicles in sight. He remarked, "Your elephant spirit, *Gajendra*[2], blessed us, madam." I agree with his sentiment.

Being in the presence of these magnificent creatures is a form of my *Seva*—my service. They are 'my living deities.' I know that even when I am not with them, they're still very much present in their elephantine way. Their energy completely covers and shields me.

The staff and mahouts often tease me, suggesting, "Why don't you just take her and keep her on your terrace?" Sometimes, I do wish it were that simple to take her out for a night or a weekend, but elephants are enormous beings. It's not as easy as taking any other animal for a brief outing. Also, it wouldn't be fair to Leela because she requires ample space, though she would be happy. So, this is Leela, my beloved Leela *Kutti*[3], my little one, my *chunkamma*[4].

My niece has grown up hearing stories about elephants. She knows them well because she has formed a good connection with them. Even though she hasn't met them physically, her love for wildlife and elephants at such a young age is heartwarming. These stories give me hope that more children will grow up with them and that future generations will be inspired by the awe and fascination for elephants, becoming compassionate decision-makers as a result.

Journey Onwards

"Safety is not just the absence of threat; safety is the presence of connection."

– Dr. Stephen Porges

The journey has also come with its challenges akin to any task in life.

Leela has had her triggers, especially with some new staff or visitors, who try to get friendly too soon. Not all of us have a rapport with them. It's important to mention that elephants are very clear about whether or not they want to interact with you. Even some of our elephants aren't keen on connecting and are happier with their elephant herd and/or human family, which is perfectly okay. When we learn to respect their boundaries, it makes life easier for everyone.

When an elephant is triggered or anxious, it is best to give them space and stay at a distance. That's what we did with Leela, as well. It was tough for both of us to be apart from each other, but it's how we learn the right way of being and communicating.

What I want to highlight is her ability to recognise my sadness. I sense she detects my distress—be it physical or emotional, too!

In one instance, I was sitting outside her shed, and there were other mahouts around. As I started talking to them, she just walked away. Like a little child, she turned her back. I felt her mahout picked up that she was angry, and suggested we go for a walk or be with her. She wants my full attention first, and once she's satisfied, she's okay with me interacting with others- humans or elephants. Otherwise, she used to smash my personal items. I've lost count of how many water bottles she has broken.

After returning from my post-recovery period, I discovered Leela had a new mahout. He was a much more reflective person and was with another elephant before. He expressed, "Oh, I am with Leela, the way you are, as in a gentle and the relational way." I couldn't be happier. We captured a beautiful image of the three of us—Leela, myself, and the mahout feeding her *kuchre* (elephant food).

As I mentioned before, it's important to note that she may have projected on me as the mother, and I see her as a child, but I also understand to not be an over-cocooning mother. I know she needs others and is starting to form new relationships.

Leela got into a timid state, as there were other elephants who were newly being rescued. Witnessing the hierarchy being established among the older elephants perhaps scared her. There was a point where she wanted either me or the mahout all the time. In a slow manner, she is engaging now with other elephants, in her own way. We are hopeful of witnessing her transformation into a true elephant, and it brings me great joy.

When people say you have this wonderful relationship, and like I earlier mentioned, it comes with a responsibility. Similar to a human mother, you cannot keep the child to yourself, as it does not aid their growth.

Most gratifying is seeing her coming to herself, accepting the place as her new home, especially considering she spent 20 years in a cramped city shed with her previous mahout. When he suddenly left, it was hugely traumatic for her once again, post her early separation from her mother. Now she is beginning to connect with others around her. This shows how building a relationship with trust and patience is most rewarding, even with elephants.

"I have had the pleasure and the privilege to follow the process of Dr. Sridhar's bonding with the heavily traumatised young elephant Leela for some years. It is with great respect and wonder about how deep and meaningful their contact has become. How soulful their communications, both verbal and non-verbal, resonates in both of them. It gives insight into the important coexistence with animal life, as it makes us emotionally and spiritually identify with nature—our own and the nature of the universe."—Lisbet Myers, Senior Jungian Analyst and Supervisor.

I would also like to put emphasis, as I did in the Palakapya Chapter, on the impact of stress on elephants. I want to stress upon what happens to elephants when they are separated from their herd, particularly the mother. Elephants, and especially females, form lifelong bonds and stay together. Sadly, with Leela, we suspect she experienced separation from her mother before the age of two, which severely impacted her socialisation.

Her human-like vocalisation is a clear sign of mimicking humans. As endearing as it looks, it's unfortunate and sad, from her context. One can only imagine the despair that must have afflicted her when her mahout, with whom she had a strong bond for 20 years, cut off all ties. It was a severe letdown and traumatising.

I became her safe space, the only connection to her previous life, and that's where it really aided, though I still wonder about our bond. I believe that we co-regulate each other.

I recall one of the U.S. veterinarians asking me, "Have you ever been scared of her?" Not after we took to each other. But I remember at the beginning, when the mahouts were so sure that they could entrust her with me, I was clueless, to be honest. I never suspected she would do anything to me, but I thought, "Really?"

Earlier, when she's been triggered, I would approach her carefully. What I first see is, "Is she connecting and responding to me?" If she's in a disconnected space, we provide her with whatever she needs, such as food and water, without close proximity and allow her to settle down.

Even when triggered most of the time, it is essential to bring them (animal or human) back to a regulated state. That's where depth psychology and poly-vagal theory have greatly helped me. It's about those connections which bring safety, creating that secure space, also known as the 'vessel' in-depth psychology.

Also, I wonder, what are we doing? What is the need to overpower an animal as magnificent as the elephant, the largest land mammal? A sense of inflation, perhaps. What are we compensating for within ourselves?

Hence, emphasising on this aspect, which I touched upon in the Palakapya chapter, the elephant Messiah—the elephant doctor. Gay Bradshaw, an American psychologist and ecologist, delved into PTSD (post-traumatic stress disorder) and depression in her book— 'Elephants on the Edge: What Animals' Teach Us About Humanity'. I am certain this 'little one' also hit on all that during her separation.

In fact, rescuing is just the first step. The journey begins by getting them to safety at a sanctuary. One never knows how much more time would go on their healing journey. It could be a few years before they settle in fully. Let's be mindful of—do we need to do this to our own heritage species? Suparna Ganguly makes a poignant plea, *"the message of captive elephants is simple and beautiful: nothing replaces nature and beloved relatives. Certainly, a message of wisdom for humanity itself."*

I often wonder about the early years of my little one. What was she like as a child? Because I remember one of my senior trainers visited and she confirmed what I always hinged upon, that psychologically, this little one was still a child and was just growing up. This was clear from the beginning, as she would always stick close to me.

I would spend time reading a book, playing music, singing to her, and she would wander off a little and begin playing in the mud. She'd venture out and break down little things, tree barks, which was a sign that she was slowly settling. Play, just like humans, means the individual is settling and is not in an overly dysregulated mode (Winnicott, 1965).

I encourage you to take notice of the next opportunity you visit an elephant camp or have the chance to see them in their natural habitat. Please show them more respect and observe from a distance.

I am not a big fan of going on many safaris. I am content seeing the ones I am with and meeting others in different camps. Do we need to disturb them all the time? Can we see them from afar? Can we respect them by leaving them alone?

The recently launched robotic elephants possess the same energy and aura we perceive when observing a real elephant, whether in the wild, in a temple, or in an institution. Play with these, not the captive ones, so the wild can stay free and the future generations can still be enamoured by the gentle giants.

I wonder, what does Leela want as a young 20-year-old elephant? What would she be doing if she were living with her herd? Perhaps she would have her own child.

If I were her elephant mother, what would I wish for her? What do I wish for her now? I want her to be truly happy, as best as possible. I am glad she is no longer in the institution, but it is still not the ideal life of freedom in the wild. This sentiment is echoed in a thought-provoking short documentary film in Kannada—titled 'Flying Elephants - The Mother's Hope'.

People often ask me, or wonder, what I do with the elephants and how I aid in their rehabilitation. To quote Marian Dunlea, author and creator of BodyDreaming, "Meeting Leela for the first time you shared a certain innocence, you came to meet her without an agenda or 'know-how'—and you waited for her to choose, to initiate the contact and how it would unfold. You responded intuitively, like the mother with her baby, attuned to her queues, vocals and actions. A world of connection and deep healing happened between you."

Robert Bosnak, my Jungian trainer and Embodied Imagination creator, speaks of 'Entrainment', which involves a deep synchronisation between hearts. It absolutely fits in with what I've believed of being attuned to Leela and the field.

To reiterate, Leela is my living goddess, with whom I have a deep, deep bond, and I respect where she is, what she is, what she brings to us and our world.

She's one of the main reasons I am writing this book so that many more Leela's do not go into oblivion. Perhaps this is her mission in this lifetime, and maybe it is through my voice.

I end this section on this note, where my little one, when it's time for me to leave, goes into her shed, puts her head down and chews fodder, knowing that I will come back the following week. Our farewells are not as difficult as before because now she has found a home! Though of late, she chooses to not follow me to her shed when I am leaving the sanctuary but retires to her place in her own time.

When I broke my leg and couldn't go for close to three months, I would initially make video calls, and she would listen, look around for me and rumble. But after a point, she would go away. I wondered, why? Later, I understood it was difficult for her to not have me physically present.

The first time I revisited, she caressed me, incessantly vocalised and rumbled, like she could feel my actual physical discomfort, and I began truly healing that day.

Also, our dear older one, who I feel is the matriarch, kept reaching out. Despite my having given her the fruits, she didn't go away, though she is a real foodie. These beautiful souls were all holding me, enabling me to come back, to heal, to emerge stronger. I feel blessed, humbled, and forever will be of service to the elephants. Hope this story has sparked your curiosity about these lovely beings.

* * *

Notes

1. **Shamanism**: Ancient spiritual practice where shamans mediate between humans and the spirit world, often linked to nature and spirit.

2. **Gajendra**: In Hinduism, Gajendra is a significant figure in the mythological story of Gajendra Moksha, in the Bhagavata Purana.
3. **Kutti**: A Kannada word meaning "little one" or "child," often used for children.
4. **Chunkamma**: Similar to Kutti.

Chapter 6

ELEPHANT TOTEM ~ SYMBOL OF THE HIGHER SELF

Image Source: Sanchi Stupa, Madhya Pradesh

"What is the function and connotation of these majestic beings that they are found in relics since time immemorial."
– **Henrich Zimmer,**
Myths and Symbols of Indian Civilisation

Elephant Symbolism. What is the need for symbolism? There are many who say, "I do not believe in such representations." What really is a symbol? Why do we require it in our lives?

Jung asserts the vital need for a symbol, specifically a new one. As we have concretised, the old, akin to what we have done with the beautiful, gracious, gentle giants, believed to be the avatar of Ganesha. Elephants are seen as the bearers of the universe, essential to our world's existence and bringing good fortune. Their statues and figurines grace our homes, in our lives, so much so that they have been literally brought, captured, tortured from the wild for reverence and entertainment.

But is that really what a symbol represents? How beautiful it is to observe an elephant, whether it be a magnificent bull or a nurturing mother with her calf. Their tender gaze and exquisite beauty bring immense joy when they are in their natural habitat.

As symbols, elephants visit us in our dreams and as totems, they hold magical energy since ancient times. In totems, even the great *Ashoka*[1] placed an elephant, which seemed to emerge from a rock-cut stone, as a symbol of peace. Animal communicators believe that they enhance the vibration of the planet. Take a moment to reflect on your own association with these magnificent creatures.

So, what exactly do they bring? Why do we need to chain them and keep them captive? This is the fundamental question that needs to be addressed.

In this chapter on the elephant totem, let us look at these facets. Akin to Airavata, the elephantine energy, Ganesha, Gajalakshmi, and how this helps us evolve and lift our consciousness. May we learn to work with the spirit and not bring them in their physical form, as they're not naturally suited to live in human habitats.

May we remember that their glory is to be free and wild, and our glory will be to aid and respect the species with what they truly deserve—freedom.

Soul of the Wild

I'd like to begin with a little guided imagery. Envision a beautiful, gracious matriarch leading the herd, which comprises a very young calf who is being adored by its mother and allomothers- the older females, including siblings—who help raise the calf. Truly, a beautiful example of bringing up a young one. They notice the matriarch is moving quicker, and they match her steps, echoing the vibration of our planet. Can you feel your heartbeat synchronised with the majestic footsteps of the elephants? Notice how your body responds to the rhythmic march of these gentle giants.

Now, I invite you to recall your own memories, whether it be of the matriarch or any other elephant you have encountered in the wild or through documentaries or videos. Take a moment to pay attention to every detail and feature as you construct a vivid image in your imagination. What aspects of the elephant are you drawn to? Is it their trunk, their sturdy and steady feet, their flapping ears, or their mischievous glee? Gradually, take in the entire body of the elephant, including its lovely tail and gracious walk, commonly known as "the Elephant Walk."

Perhaps witnessing quietly from afar just how they navigate their surroundings. To be around them is magical. As you immerse yourself in this beautiful scene, what sensations do you experience? Can you sense your breath returning to your body, the ground under your feet, held by Mother Earth? Rooted and yet uplifted by the presence of these magnanimous beings.

Now, shift your focus to the trunk. How does it appear? What do you sense? The trunk, with its remarkable features and diverse capabilities, is astounding. From sucking water to picking up a tiny little grain that's fallen and so delicately, it can swish away a fly, dust itself with mud, spray water, and reach upwards. Sensing, hearing, feeling.

I would like you to try to see if you can imitate and perform this action. First, when the trunk is in its natural position, it can reach down and touch the earth, connecting with her and our mother. Then, if you slowly raise it up, it can reach high above thanks to its immense size and height. As you perform this action, pay attention to what happens to you. What and how are you feeling?

The trunk is very alive to me and resonates at the heart level, making it a living symbol. Contemplating the symbolism of the Divine elephant has led me to engage with it meaningfully as a holding totem. We will delve deeper into this topic as we continue with this chapter.

Originally, my intention was to first introduce a Totem, but then the elephantine energy took over and guided me to bring in this vivid imagery and reflection.

In 2021, during a discussion with my Jungian supervisor Lauren Cunningham, I shared an epiphany I had while reading the book about body dreaming. I realised the trunk has always been alive, vivid and holding for me. Echoing Dr. Bedi's quote on the elephant, which holds both, and connects—the cosmic and the earth.

Later on, the trunk came alive in my description of Leela reaching out to me. Elephants also reach out to others gracefully with their trunks. Have you noticed how they use their trunks to connect, express joy, soothe other herd members, friends or young ones?

Sacred World

I recently came across a beautiful video of the Sheldrick Wildlife Trust, where orphaned elephants are rescued and rewilded. The video showed young calves suckling their keeper's thumb. It is extremely essential to have such a bond until they become secure. Eventually, they form bonds with other elephants within the sanctuary. When they are ready, they spread their wings and slowly return to the wild. It's a remarkable process of rewilding.

Even my little one, Leela, consistently reaches out her trunk to me. It's her way of connecting. I hold her trunk, whisper her name, blow into it, and tell her I love her. I can hear her vocals and the low rumbles, and that's the authentic connection from her trunk to my heart. My heart expands as I envision this scene every single time.

Let's look at this a little deeper. Reaching out to another, in this case, me, represents the horizontal axis, while the connection to the ground and the heavens represents the vertical axis. In this way, the trunk becomes alive as the symbol of the centre of the universe, of the *axis mundi*, which is the central point of the universe.

Is it surprising? As Indians, we know about the *Chakra System*[2]. Airavata, or the elephant, is in the ground or *root chakra*[3], which is also connected to the elephant-headed God Ganesha.

During a recent seminar by Steven Hermann, a Jungian Analyst and author with extensive connections to both the East and West, he delved into the concept of the interconnected facets, focusing specifically on the elephant ground. This particular discussion resonated deeply, given my recent experience of losing a cherished elder elephant.

When Steven spoke about the concept of elephant grounding, which I had specifically requested, it appeared as though the spirit of our dear elephant was holding me. The term "elephant ground" refers to the grounding energy that emanates from these magnificent creatures.

Even within our own culture and customs, particularly Swami Vivekananda, a visionary thinker, along with other saints, emphasised the concept of *Samyama*[4]—a state of equilibrium achieved through, 'holding the image of the elephant'. That's what elephants are—enormous yet gentle creatures who could aid our meditation too!

Their remarkable agility allows them to move so silently that at times, I am unaware of their presence until they are right beside me or behind me. Observing elephants in a tranquil environment, whether in the wild or in a sanctuary, has a grounding and meditative effect. People who have witnessed these moments, including those who have watched my videos, often speak about the transformative experience it offers. Even one of our senior trainers, who visited recently, was profoundly moved and experienced a sense of rejuvenation akin to a retreat.

It's like being in this beautiful waterfall that refreshes and rejuvenates you, and you're held so dearly by the gracious, beautiful elephants (from afar).

A sudden insight into the elephant ground sprung on me whilst developing a template for this chapter. This is my interpretation; I offer it for your reflection. Airavata, the divine elephant, is holding/carrying us at the base (root chakra). So, we are literally sitting on top of the elephant, just like Ganesha, the remover of obstacles.

Elephants, as we know, are the universe's caryatids. As we discussed in a previous chapter, they hold our universe. Perhaps this ancient knowing, the deep cellular memory, beckons us to be with the spirit of the elephant.

However, we must question whether we are mistaken in wanting the real elephant to serve us. Do we merely desire to sit on top of it, go for a ride, and seek its blessings? Is that even necessary? Perhaps we seek the elephant's depths and its consciousness to guide us. These are significant reflections that call for our thoughtful contemplation before we take any action.

At this juncture, I'd like to introduce the concept of a symbol. A symbol is an image or concept arising from the depths of our consciousness. It has multiple meanings and can be a bridge to a higher state. Therefore, symbols and totems hold the numinous energy.

Throughout the book and our cultural associations, we have come to realise that elephants have always been revered for their divinity. Sadly, we have mistreated these majestic creatures, breaking their spirits. We have subjected them to torture, encroached upon their habitats, and reduced them to mere puppets - even in our acts of rituals.

This begs the question: what happens behind the scenes? How equipped are we to maintain hordes of elephants in cramped places? Do we even need to do so? Have we misunderstood and misinterpreted the symbol? Perhaps, in our quest to concretise a symbol, we have inadvertently stripped it of its divine essence, reducing it to a mere sign.

This may be why I was guided to first take you through the imaginative journey of the elephant and its trunk. I encourage you to sit with this and reflect on your inner experience, what resonates and restricts. What is more beautiful: a free elephant in the wild, in its natural habitat, where it belongs, or the one tied up in shackles, broken in spirit, alone, dissociated amidst scores of humans but not their herd.

Do chained or captive elephants give us joy?

As Carl Jung asserts, *"A living symbol speaks to us."* There are countless interpretations, and one can never know, just like we can never fully grasp the vastness of the universe or of God.

What is it that our culture requires and the symbol that we need to birth? What attitude must die in order for a new mindset, akin to Ganesha's head, which embodies the elephant (animal) and the human consciousness? Transpersonal self—the unity in all its aspects.

Symbolic Life

Let us now look at the emerging elephant, or what I refer to as the emerging elephant, in the Kalinga district of Orissa. When you visit the place or see its image, this elephant appears to be emerging from the stone structure. Some sources suggest that it is reminiscent of how a white elephant entered *Queen Mahamaya*[5] before the birth of Buddha, hence he is referred to as 'the greatest of elephants'—*Gajotama*[6].

The structure was built after the *Kalinga War*[7], a war of extreme bloodshed that transformed Ashoka. In that transformative phase of his awakening, he embraced Buddhism. An emerging elephant, a symbol of hope and peace, stands as a protector of the space, making for an auspicious sign. For Ashoka, through the elephant totem, was also inviting the energy of auspiciousness, protection of the noble and standing for what is right. The honourable values that an elephant embodies and signifies.

The image has remained vivid in my memory. We can also see the reverberation of the Palakapya legend with elephants' transformative energy reflected here. The elephants symbolise hope, perhaps claiming their divinity and elevating ours! They save us from destruction now, just as sage Palakapya saved them. Guardians of the world and our soul, indeed!

Elephant icons found in temples and art throughout Asia are symbolic. It invites us to go within and allow it to shift something deep within us. If only we pause and pay attention, be it our own heritage sites, temples, especially *Ellora Caves*[8], 'the elephantine caves of Ellora', the shift will begin to happen. Can we tap into the subtle energy which is moving the universe? The elephants, literally, hold and support the universe/cosmos.

Their trunk serves as a connection between heaven and earth, recalling stories of their celestial origins as a guiding map to our consciousness.

Regardless of one's belief in these tales, elephants remain a special species that we may never fully understand. However, I hope it will not be too late to protect them, as their presence among us enables our own inner growth, well-being, society and humanity at large.

As I delve deeper into this chapter and consider what to convey, I am moved by the realisation that this book is not just about elephants; it is also about our own selves. This sentiment, shared by one of my trainers, is becoming increasingly evident as I progress with this project.

Now, I would also like to introduce Tara, the elephant, who is described by Mark Shand, a travel writer and conservationist, in his book 'Travels on my elephant'. He explains how his encounter with Tara led him to become a conservationist and support the elephant movement. According to Shand, it is possible to fall in love with a place, an animal, or a person. He says, "I fell in love with India and with Tara, the elephant". The reason I bring up Tara here is that throughout their journey, she refused to enter a certain place, sensing the remnants of her ancestors who were involved in a war which we will re-touch in the final segment.

Discovering the Numinous

Jung talks about 'a living symbol' and 'a dying symbol'. A living symbol is what holds the *numen*[9], as I mentioned earlier. It is the spark and you just know, like when you had a dream, or an epiphany, or in your reverie and you even find it synchronously. The energy is alive and throbbing. You can never say, "This is exactly what it is," because the moment you think this is 'it' (meaning), we reduce it to a mere sign.

Unfortunately, it seems that this is what we have done to the elephant—concretised it and abused it for our needs. Nowhere in any scripture does it say that the elephant needs to perform rituals. Elephants are often donated by devotees, which even places a burden on the institutions that care for them. In fact, some temples are struggling to provide for their elephants because it is a difficult task, especially evident during Covid.

There is a proverb in *Kannada*[10] that goes like this, 'taking care of an elephant' which signifies a humongous task. This is especially true for captive elephants who often suffer from physical issues because they are not meant to live in captivity or serve as domestic pets. They can never be completely tamed, and this is precisely why we witness many concerns, instances of abuse, deaths, and conflicts surrounding them.

When mahouts are not well equipped, they do not read the signs well. But how could we blame them? After all, the elephants are not supposed to be sticking to us. I am using the word 'sticking' because coexistence does not mean we have to be in each other's face. Even in any relationship, there needs to be some space. Without it, things start to become suffocating.

When we consider the elephant and other wild species, not every species is meant to be domesticated like dogs or cats. Domestication brings immense suffering to them, and if we truly touch our hearts, suffering to our own self.

Let's pause and I will guide you through this vivid image; or, more precisely, this realm of imagination. Imagine an elephant calf. I am sure most of us have seen videos of them at least once. It's a pure delight to witness a newborn's first attempts to stand, a crucial step taken within hours of birth, much like every other animal in the animal kingdom. One of the most fascinating aspects of the calf is the trunk, which has around 40,000 muscles. It's quite a challenge for the calf to navigate and figure out how to use it.

As I write this, I find myself shaking my head in disbelief. Picture this beautiful little calf, running joyously among the herd. Its tiny trunk is busy figuring out how to suckle, drink water, and how to control it. Take a moment to notice what you feel and how it impacts you.

I have witnessed both ends of the spectrum.

Now, visualise a calf born amidst humans in an institution. I am about to describe a scene that I saw. The mother is tethered and tied, with another elephant providing support. While the calf is free to roam, but instead of being surrounded by its elephant family and the herd, it sees humans, although only a few. The calf is excited, but the mother remains vigilant. How does this affect the little calf? Because the mother is tethered, it can only stay within a very narrow boundary/space.

Just picture the mother of both calves' emotional state.

If we put ourselves in their position for a brief moment, what would we prefer to see? A free calf in the wild, surrounded by its herd, or an undeniably adorable calf missing out on the wonders of the wild, the support of the allomothers, and the companionship of the herd, all due to our desires and whims?

We have discussed this extensively, but I wanted to reiterate that we are focusing on the symbol itself.

May we hold the numinous, the living symbol, the energy that an elephant brings, so that it does not become a dying symbol, or worse, the extinction of an entire species.

Can we hold the 'hope' in the current times? As suggested by the Kalinga edict and sacred architecture. We ought to withdraw our projections and stop keeping elephants in captivity. They are the caryatids and pillars of the earth. If we tune in and understand their symbolism, we wouldn't want to keep them amidst us—in institutions for rituals or entertainment. Their purpose is greater than that. Instead, let's hold them in our hearts, not bound in chains away from their own kind. Free from the curse, soaring upward happily!

In Jungian terms, when we hold the two polarities, a new third emerges. The tension between opposites, and the remarkable emergence we are witnessing now, is the creation of robotic elephants—a creative shift and healing spirit, embodying the elephantine spirit/energy.

Image Source: Hampi, Karnataka, India

Wisdom Keepers

I was fortunate to be invited to the unveiling of the robotic elephants in one of the government temples in Karnataka (*Muzrai*[11]). Previously, this place had housed an elephant that endured immense suffering. The elephant was kept in solitary confinement, practically confined to a cage-like structure until it succumbed to its condition. However, she found solace in her last few moments or months in a sanctuary surrounded by loved ones of her own kind.

As I witnessed the sheer excitement and the joy that the robotic elephant was bringing, I was remembering the real elephant and the destiny she carried. Hopefully, the fate of many other elephants will not be the same. May we embrace more of the robotic as our *Sanātana*

Dharma[12] teaches us to empower and care for all beings. This would be a true homage and not contradict anything.

During the writing of this book, I synchronously discovered and read 'The Surrender Experiment'. Interestingly, it has been with me since last year. It spoke about the jail inmates and how they could hold or come to their centre, through ritual, meditation, and the support of the Sangha or community. An inner freedom beyond anyone's reach. It occurred to me that this same principle and its potential may apply to war-torn countries, prisoners of war, and even captive animals.

Given our own experiences during the COVID pandemic, one can't help but remember how we were confined to a metaphorical golden cage. The impact of the virus on our lives was profound. It forced us to question whether it was the virus that disturbed our ecology or if we were the ones responsible for disturbing the delicate balance of nature. Perhaps the virus was merely shaking us up and making us aware of the havoc we have been wreaking on the planet and its precious species. The final section on sacred ecology will explore these themes further.

Now, if you're curious about the way forward, it is a thought worth reflecting upon. As we say in sports, "Move from problem to solution."

Thinking about this, I just remembered *Appu*, 'the sports mascot'! Do you recall him? Appu was the mascot of the 1982 Asian Games, and his image has stayed in our memories, especially for those of us involved in sports. He was a bubbly adorable elephant with a red *tilak* (a mark, generally made on the centre of the forehead) symbolising friendship and fraternity forever. Apparently, he led the contingent. There are also sources suggesting that this mascot was inspired by a real elephant, although we cannot verify the truth of this claim.

What is heartening is that the mascot was used instead of subjecting a young elephant calf to intensive training and breaking, just for our entertainment. Appu Ghar, an amusement park, sparked my interest in playing with words and reminiscing about sitting with a temple elephant. It made me ponder if we could replace the term "temple elephant" with "divine elephant," as we often see elephants depicted in sacred architecture like the Ellora Caves and other ancient heritage sites.

Gajavana—Where Elephants once roamed Free

In ancient India, *Gajavana*—protected 'elephant forests'—were dedicated sanctuaries where elephants roamed freely under state care. This term finds its earliest mentions in *Kautilya's Arthashastra* (Sukumar, 2011), long before wildlife conservation became a global concern. The forests balanced conservation with practicality, ensuring their well-being and making them worthy of respectful living on this planet. Passionate researchers of Asian Elephants' history, highlights how Gajavana shaped human-elephant relationships and co-existence. Reviving these ancient concepts and blending them with modern wildlife protection might be a way forward to restore harmony and move away from the commodification of our so-called Gods.

In this context, *Appu Ghar*, or *Ghar Appu*, could be interpreted as the true home or sanctuary for elephants, resembling a forest. It intrigues me to think about the concept of an elephant temple, where these magnificent creatures are revered and the forests are honoured, just as our ancestors did. Perhaps future generations will develop a deep admiration for elephants and continue to protect them.

I vaguely recall a story about a young boy who grew up in the forest, nurtured by the animals and especially the Matriarch. However, when humans found him, they attempted to capture him. As he grows older, he carries a subconscious memory of his time with the elephants.

One day, he has a dream of the elephant herd bathing and enjoying themselves in a river. Eventually, the Matriarch signals for them to leave, and they vanish into a secret place unknown to humans—the elephant temple.

Maybe it's just my imagination or a dream, but I wish they had their own spaces and temples, similar to the elephant grave. I hope there are places we can't access, known only to them, which is their safe haven. Somewhere in the forest, hidden in the waters, away from human eyes. A place entirely their own, where their space is secure, the planet belonging to them.

As I bring this chapter to a close, I feel more settled and hopeful that the symbol is coming alive. In fact, as I mentioned elsewhere, when the elephants entered my life, the Gajalakshmi Totem appeared synchronously, signalling that the goddess is calling, emerging. Are we listening? Are we ready? Shall we open our doors? Our hearts? We'll touch more on Gajalakshmi in the final chapter on Anima Mundi—World Soul.

The dream we discussed earlier has come to my mind once again. I envision a little girl walking hand in trunk with the beautiful elephant, the gigantic, so very gently holding her, she's so little, yet at par with the mighty giant.

It makes me wonder if we, as humans, can strive for such harmony. Must we always assert our dominance and try to tame these magnificent creatures? I believe elephants possess a patience and grace that surpasses our own. Perhaps, as humans continue to evolve, we can learn from them.

I am fascinated by the image of their beautiful walk, hand in hand, hand in trunk. Remember the trunk as a living symbol? And we are all communing. The little girl and the elephant become one as they fly upward. Just thinking about it brings a smile to my face as wide as an elephant's trunk!

I ponder the message of this dream. Could it be urging us to acknowledge the elephants' rightful place on Earth and restore their divinity in the heavens? Perhaps that is the message, too.

I find myself deeply humbled and honoured to have had this dream and to be able to share it with you, the readers, and the collective consciousness. As a collective, may we dream, may we re-member and rebirth a new symbol, or the symbol which needs en-livening. So, these gracious, magnanimous beings continue to be on our precious planet and in our lives.

May we really cherish these beings, for that is my deepest desire. May we come together, and evolve for ourselves, for the species, for the earth.

I believe this is the divine purpose of the elephant.

Also, see what else comes in your reverie and fantasy, imagination and dreams, as they whisper cosmic musings through their wings, trunk, feet—their beingness. Just open to the energy and let the magic happen! 'Elephants in the clouds' has been a metaphor that has held me as I would look up to the elephant energy in the clouds, reclaiming their divine space!

* * *

Reflections

1. Contemplate on a symbol that is holding.
2. How will you engage with the Elephant Totem?
3. Has it begun to resonate?
4. Honour the guidance through dreams and synchronicities.

Notes

1. **Ashoka**: Ashoka is renowned for his significant role in the spread of Buddhism across ancient Asia after the brutal Kalinga War.
2. **Chakra System**: The chakra system is an ancient concept originating from Hinduism and Buddhism, which describes the body's energy centres.
3. **Root Chakra**: The first chakra in the human energy system, also called Muladhara, representing grounding, survival instincts, and stability.
4. **Samyama**: A meditative discipline in yoga that combines concentration (*dharana*), meditation (*dhyana*), and absorption (*samadhi*).
5. **Queen Mahamaya**: The mother of Siddhartha Gautama (the Buddha).
6. **Gajotama**: A term denoting the 'supreme elephant' or the noblest among elephants, symbolising wisdom, strength, and dignity in Indian tradition.
7. **Kalinga War**: A historic battle fought between Emperor Ashoka and the kingdom of Kalinga.

8. **Ellora Caves**: A UNESCO World Heritage Site in Maharashtra, India, known for its rock-cut temples including carvings of elephants.
9. **Numen**: A term used to denote the spark or spiritual presence or divine power inherent in natural objects or phenomena, often evoking awe.
10. **Kannada**: A classical Dravidian language spoken predominantly by the people of Karnataka in southwestern India.
11. **Muzrai**: Refers to the temple administration system in Karnataka, which also oversees temple elephants and their welfare.
12. **Sanātana Dharma**: A term referring to the eternal, universal principles of dharma, often considered synonymous with Hinduism's spiritual and philosophical traditions.

*"In the hush between our stories,
Nature waits for our yes."*

SECTION 3
SACRED ECOLOGY

Chapter 7

RECONNECTING TO NATURE AND GAIA

Does the Earth have a soul? What about animals? Or is it just hogwash, as they call the tree huggers? Animals! Do you sense them? Maybe a deer hiding somewhere is wondering, "Has this human being awakened?" When you get a chance, pause and look into the eyes of the animal, whether that's your animal companion or a wild one. You might be touched by their oceanic depths, rekindling your own connection to the mysteries of life.

Then, you will begin to feel connected to the heartbeat of the Earth, your own self, the animal within, and the animals around, and perhaps feel part of the greater whole—a sense of oneness. 'Gaia', Mother Earth, awaits us, and so do all her beings, just as we are part of this vast, all-expanding universe. May we heed the call of the land and the longing of our own soul.—CS.

Imagine a natural space, and as you're walking in the lush green forest. Your mind begins to switch off from the mundane overthinking, and you can feel your feet kissing the Earth. The rustling of the leaves, your breath in your body, in your being. You may lie down with no worry in the world, knowing you are held by *Mother Earth*. As you tune into this ancient connection that our soul longs for, you may feel the air, the wind, the leaves, the birds calling and cooing.

"It is now my invitation to recall a nature trip from your childhood and see what it evokes. Then, if you can go down memory lane when you held an animal or witnessed a birth."

Perhaps this will bring about feelings of nostalgia or a sense of reverie. Now, think about the animal—what did it evoke in you? Did it awaken a sense of tenderness?

My journey began in the mists of the Western Ghats—nature's haven, nestled safely in my maternal grandparents' abode. I often wonder if this is the root wherein the wild in me was nurtured, nature's child in the true sense! Also, the moment I held our little dog, 'Heilo', I melted, and the instinctual mother arose in me. I feel the same way about the elephant, my 'little one', even though she was already a young adult when we first met. Guess it was in the field (energy field).

I aim to focus on the concept of reconnecting with nature in this section—both our inner and outer nature and the relatedness between the two, which greatly influences and drives our lives. It is essential to recognise that we are an integral part of nature, and when we are out of sync with its rhythms, we experience discord and disconnection from life itself. Even amidst external successes, we may feel a certain staleness, a longing to establish a relationship with the depths of our soul.

One can tune into nature by experiencing a soulful relationship with animals, too. This, in turn, allows individuals to rediscover their own alliance with nature, which we will explore later on.

Let's first begin by delving into rituals and their role in our lives and draw parallels from our older generation who seemed to live more harmoniously.

Rituals are one way that our ancients tuned into the natural rhythm of life, be it via festivals and with daily practices.

I shared with a few friends how meditative I find cycling. They reacted with disbelief as if my perspective was completely outrageous. However, this newfound perspective on cycling came about after I underwent a major knee surgery.

Cycling has become a valuable part of my daily routine. It not only helps me gain strength in my injured knee and stay fit, but it also has a positive impact on my overall well-being. Instead of whining about my injury, I learned to incorporate cycling into my day, and it has proven to be beneficial.

As I cycle, I read or meditate and reflect, thus beginning my day and prepping up to face the world. It has become a part of my daily ritual that I cherish. Being an introvert, cycling is the perfect way for me to recharge and gather energy for the marathon day that lies ahead. By being present and unrushed, I am able to fully revive and be more engaged throughout the day. On the other hand, the days when I jump out of bed and rush through the day, I find myself feeling exhausted and irritable. But when I begin the day by taking time for myself, it adds more value to myself and others.

Nada yoga[1] (a form of yoga) advises you to begin the day by tuning into the sounds within yourself, such as your heartbeat and breath.

Once you have calibrated these internal sounds, shift your attention to the sounds just outside your room. You may hear the gentle chirping of a bird, the rustling of leaves, or the scurrying of a squirrel. Finally, expand your awareness to the sounds on the road, where you might encounter the joyful sounds of children playing and the familiar hum of vehicles.

As I started practising this, I found myself attuned to the subtle rhythms, rather than just the chaotic honks of the city. Give this exercise a shot and observe what happens. You may find that your nervous system and body appreciate this added inclusion, rather than treating the body as mere machines!

In most cultures, religious rituals are often recommended to be performed early in the morning and perhaps at night, and there is a science to it. The first half hour of the day and night are natural hypnagogic states—meaning what's on your mind greatly influences your subconscious. Have you ever wondered why you struggle to sleep well after engaging in non-stop chatting, watching social media, or reading world news before bed? The reason lies in the fact that your brain wave frequency remains active and is unable to switch off.

I advise athletes that they need to get off the pressure cooker and be normal individuals post-training, thus giving their system the much-needed break. Remember *Simon Biles's*[2] tweet before she pulled out of the Tokyo Olympic finals citing 'twisties'. The gymnast stayed true to herself and later returned with the medal after a few days. Not everyone perhaps understood her tweet, saying, "It puts tremendous pressure on being tweeted by millions," especially prior to an Olympic event!

Ever wondered why we want to go to nature for a holiday, and what happens to your biological clock? In *Anam Cara*[3], John O'Donohue beautifully explains the darkest hour of the night is just before dawn. When we synchronise our system to nature, we wake up, and are productive during the day. Gradually slowing down by evening, going inward and relaxing, and finally retiring to attune to our deeper selves in our dreams and reflections. In this way, we're much more regulated than being in a sympathetic overload, driving ourselves to exhaustion.

Modern life has gone far from the natural order, and I strongly feel that we need to get simpler in our approach to life, which means making space to listen to what life is really telling us and follow suit.

Are we listening to the whispers of the cosmos and within us? There is a time to play, to work and to rest. We till the field, sow the seed and await the rains and then harvest the crops. Coming from an agricultural family, I often hear our caretakers say *"bhoomi thayi"* (*Mother Earth*) needs to rest too.

Similarly, the moon waxes and wanes, and most women would 'bleed' (menstruation cycle) around the new moon and are advised to rest. The full moon is a time of bright moonlight, and we are in an extroverted energy seeking social ties with others. Whilst the new moon (dark moon) is a time of quiet inner reflection.

I have noticed this with animals, including elephants too. It seems like they have an inner clock that is tuned into nature's rhythms. Do we even pay attention to this? If not, why not start now?

In fact, I followed a Monday ritual associated with Lord *Shiva*—my *Ishta* (favourite deity). The process of preparation started with the ritualistic bath, decorating the altar with flowers and finally the *Abhisheka*[4] had a unique ring to it. Surprisingly, I wouldn't get hungry till sunset, the time to break the fast. This ritual was a way to unite with my higher Self by focusing my energy on the deity.

Possibly, this is the reason I don't have Monday blues. On the contrary, it is one of my favourite days. The other being the weekend, when I travel to meet the Elephants as it is my service to them. Anticipating these encounters fills me with excitement, and I can't help but feel something amiss when I am unable to meet them. Spending quality time with these majestic creatures and allowing myself a much-needed rest nourishes my soul, enabling me to bring forth my best self to the world once more.

Rationalisation and Disconnection

Jung had warned us of this one-sidedness signified by over-rationalisation and a disconnect from nature. Imagine what happens when you spend the whole day staring at a screen for work or social media. Your body and mind becomes weighed down and need to recharge. Taking a break, especially if it's outdoors or having a light moment with your team/family, can make you feel refreshed and replenished.

Occasionally, I hear a client or athlete describe their day, and it is flat akin to a robot. When I reflect it to them, they are shocked. This is when we work together to establish rituals that can help them feel more engaged and alive in their daily lives.

In this era of the head, we shun away the heart and feeling as it is too much and considered weak; however, feelings thwarted or suppressed will need to be channelled if we do not want to end up with physical or mental breakdowns, which is a bane of our modern society.

Consider this young athlete who tried to be as peppy as possible and hold herself together in the session, but her dreams were about death and abandonment of dogs especially since she was an avid dog lover. Her inner nature was distressed and sought attention. Her routine was almost robotic and there was no sense of joy.

The first step was to help her rediscover the essence of life and find ways to do a little something to bring back the energy of play. Gradually, she started looking forward to volunteering visits to an animal shelter/orphanage, and it opened up her tenderness-feeling quotient. Spending time with friends and not shutting down was key.

Only when we began processing her emotions and the tears started flowing, releasing stuck energy, was there a shift in her outer life. When she initiated integrating the instinctual and living life outside the robotic mode, it lifted her depression, and she truly started living a young adult's life with all its joys and challenges. Once she reconnected to life, not surprisingly, her performance improved as well.

At this juncture, I'd like to bring in one of my favourite anecdotes from analytical psychology that Carl Jung loved to narrate, titled 'the rainmaker'. In a certain village, a severe drought loomed large. The village elders convened and called a Shaman from another village. The medicine man asked for a small hut and locked himself in it for three days, and then it started raining.

Wilhelm, who was present and narrated this story, inquired, "What did you do?" to which the Shaman replied that he didn't do anything. When he was again asked how it began to rain, he said, "This place was out of *Tao*[5] (centre), and I had to bring myself to the Tao for it to rain (as I became imbalanced on coming to this place)."

So, the Shaman did not take credit for bringing the rain but got into the right balance to influence the *field* from that state (Jung, Vision Seminars).

During my childhood, I used to hold dear a song in Malnad called *huyu huyu maleraya*, which had a unique meaning of invoking the rain gods to bring us blessings, unlike the popular 'rain-rain go away' rhyme taught in schools nowadays. The intention is to be more inclusive with nature and not to force her to dance to our tunes.

Interestingly, the Hopi tribe in Native America also has rituals running to evoke rain. Running served as a communal activity for praying and a way to bond, in addition to providing obvious health benefits.

What lessons can we extract from these stories that can be incorporated into our own lives and workplaces to uplift and empower ourselves? Are you able to flow with life and how can one come into a more balanced state of flow more often?

Undoubtedly, it is high time we reevaluate our functioning. The Covid pandemic has clearly shown how challenging it is to be isolated and disengaged from the outside world. Only animals thrived, and the air became noticeably fresher due to reduced human-induced pollution.

Reconnection to Anima Mundi or World Soul

"An Elephant is a Rain cloud walking on Earth."
— **Heinrich Zimmer**

In the seminars on nature and modern life, Jung highlights the purpose of certain mysteries, especially the *dionysian*[6] whose purpose was to direct people back to the animal—the inner animal—to our instinct.

We've gotten so much in our heads that we need to find our way back to the instinct as well, which our ancient ancestors were in sync with and used to survive amidst natural threats and calamities.

In fact, those of us who are privileged to have animal companions (rather than merely calling them pets) or work for them, understand via the senses and instinct primarily, as we attune to the energy field. The trunk caretakers (mahouts) especially say one must observe and gauge through intuition, as there isn't so much time to rationalise and it can be dangerous if we are inflated by thinking only from the head.

Animals play a very important role in our relation to nature and aid our healing as well, including our animal companions and domestic animals. Have you ever wondered at the time an animal came into your life? Were you going through some shifts or challenges? How did they aid you? I'd urge you to ponder this aspect.

In my case, the animals, including the elephants, have come at pivotal junctures, including holding dreams at major transitions. For example, I dreamt of a large herd coming to greet me when I was in quarantine during the Covid bio-bubble of IPL, 2020, held in Dubai. Being amidst an all-male team in uncertain times was challenging. The dream held and made me feel safe in the new space. It was almost like the herd were my cheerleaders, thereby providing me comfort and strength, which then helped me hold the team in a safe psychological space. I felt a lot more connected to myself and my inner power animal. Thus, the elephant herd was rooting for me and the team I was working with.

I feel tender, writing this section as I realise how much I've been supported by the Elez (as we call them), even when I have been far away from them. Dr. Porges speaks of and co-regulating, by mirroring, and calming each other's nervous system with authentic connections. By delving into the soul of the animal, we are attuned to their spirit, which reaches out to us in our quiet sacred dream space. I've also felt the holding energy of Heilo (my bratty dog) many times who transitioned (passed away).

Dr. Porges asserts that these deep relations rewire our brain and neural pathways, which is what therapy also does aiding healing. It seems this is the reason we have therapy dogs and equestrian therapy. As long as the animals are comfortable and willing, without us solely using them only to meet our ends.

By now, you might have a glimpse into the rituals and the powerful bonds individuals create with the natural world. But let's go beyond that and observe how honouring the ancestor's ritual also involves their uplifted energy. When we give them space, we are respecting the ongoing process of life and nature. Personally, I am in awe of what is emerging in this section as I open myself to reconnection—which is essential in honouring our land, ancestors, and all species. It is a momentous occasion that encompasses the entirety of life.

Animals help us understand our emotions as we bond from a heart-centred space. This may also bring up some emotions that need processing and help us release stuck energy and channel them. You must have noticed how animals shake their body as a way of releasing; body-centred therapies highly suggest movement and shaking to release pent-up energy. Pay attention to how your animal friend also senses your mood and energy quite accurately.

Furthermore, psychological studies have shown that animal abusers most likely will become more violent and harm the society if they aren't provided the right support, and work towards resolving their issues.

In fact, I feel the restlessness that is often diagnosed as ADHD (a neuro-developmental disorder) is the release that youngsters often need from an overly rigid system. For young athletes, I recommend encouraging playtime, particularly outdoors in the park and barefoot whenever feasible, to calm their restless minds and promote freedom from constant control. This has seen a significant re-channelling of their excess energy. A coach's son was referred for aggression issues, but what he truly required was a way to direct his energy into productive activities.

It is high time for our system to re-look at more natural, empowered ways of education that cater to mind, body and soul!

Are children or adults, for that matter, meant to stay in closed walls an entire day? Our one-sided pursuit of success has caused more harm and ungrounded individuals. Society's preoccupation with growth and expansion has caused us to separate ourselves from nature and the individuals around us. Society wrongly assumes it can treat animals in the same manner, resulting in their mistreatment and the heartbreaking separation from their families, as we see with captive elephants.

We've all had that experience of entering a picturesque green landscape, where the air feels refreshingly crisp, and a light dew paints the surroundings. The sheer joy of feeling the water on your skin and watching the waves crash on an uncrowded beach is truly unparalleled. The sensation of the ground beneath our feet or the soothing touch of water or being able to listen to birds perhaps, or an animal, can transport us into a surreal state.

Now think of the sound of blaring traffic being stuck in this urban jungle. You're jolted suddenly. Unfortunately, I don't know what an urban jungle is, but it appears to shut us off. Because we are part of nature, and when we choose to disconnect, whether consciously or unconsciously, there's bound to be discord.

There's a yearning to be part of life and belong to the natural world. After all, we came from here and will return, eventually.

When I am with elephants, I feel a deep unity. Spending time with them means being more present and away from the phone, which is a great way to beingness. We have all experienced this state, even with our animal companions. All they want is our presence. They communicate subtly through their eyes and body language, but do we actively pay attention and listen? Even when we are angry or they have done something wrong, how quickly they acknowledge it, recognise what's done and innocently come back to us.

Besides with elephants, I think the magnanimity of their being, their sheer size, the way they move, the unhurried pace except when there's a place to go to or they've put their mind on getting a fruit for example, nothing can stop them. Just observing them—the way they reach out to each other, even to their human companions is a treat to watch and endless joy. Bathing, playing, mud bathing, trumpeting, doing trunk ballet. You can sit and observe them for hours and hours. There's something so magical about being in that space. I am someone who would get lost even within nature, so it is not at all surprising that these beings really tug at my heartstrings. And my little one makes me feel I am her world!

This is not just my experience. We all desire harmony, which is why many of us crave to get away from the city on holidays. However, this can lead to disturbing wildlife when large numbers of people visit, disturbing the natural landscape and peace.

Do we ever wonder how our actions impact us? It is a lot easier to blame the forest department, but wildlife isn't seeking to come to the city unless we leave them no choice. Our actions are contradictory— first, we clear away our greenery, but then we go chase the greenery and for conflict and enter the human areas because of the deforestation caused by our pursuit of growth and urbanisation. Karnataka Forest Minister, Eshwar Khandre must be applauded for supporting the Forest Department in taking crucial steps for wildlife. One such step was to restrict the number of trekkers entering natural terrains and overcrowding the place during holidays.

How do we positively impact and influence the ecosystem? Perhaps we can begin by creating a small garden, a small sanctuary space for ourselves within our own homes.

Earlier, I would feel a dissonance when I had to leave natural spaces during retreats or nature holidays. I would literally feel like my soul was ripped apart while leaving the place. Gradually, I learned to integrate the experience and hold nature within me. It is not possible to be with elephants all the time, but I can now hold them by being able to connect to the spaces and to their energy. My room and altar also have a sacred space so I can connect to the Elephants. It's worth reflecting on how our current home and work environments are structured, and what small changes we can make to incorporate more greenery and natural space for our well-being.

Stephen Harding, in his book on *Animate Earth*, advised to create a little space and ritual to reconnect to nature (*Gaia*).

I've tried doing this with athletes, especially those who are in their heads all the time and are chronic overthinkers. Building simple rituals, like having their morning cup of tea outside or taking a walk in the garden, is helpful. Athletes are advised to avoid headphones when they go for a walk. Instead, to be open to the enchanting melodies of birds and the harmonious symphony of nature, as it is full of life. We may fail to appreciate these little joys if we're preoccupied with our thoughts or engrossed in music.

What is the point of going for a walk if we are going to focus just on a particular piece of music? In fact, the whole walk can indeed regulate our nervous system, because we are looking around and seeing varied colours, which also prevents tunnel vision. This way we can listen to a bird call or song and allow ourselves to be in the moment. Research also supports this theory.

I remember my own safe haven and the comfort of my grandparents' home in Malnad. Early in the morning, my granny would delicately adorn herself. Only then presented herself, first to her garden, tending with great care just as she would with us all.

We would run to collect the *parijata*—night jasmine flowers, as my grandfather would await us and shake the tree. Many more tiny flowers would caress us gently, which we gleefully attempted to collect on our clothes. It felt like Mother Nature loved our little game and smiled at us. We are her children too! Then play with the butterflies and dash for a simple yet soulfully prepared breakfast.

I have often wondered about the contentment of my grandparents, which percolated us all. A small house amidst a bigger garden with bougainvillaea in abundance, just the way it ought to be. Signifying we are part of the larger scheme of things in nature. Moderation and balance are the themes echoed by *Kuvempu*, Malnad's own poet who deeply impacted our young minds and hoping it does so with many more generations.

The pleasant memories of childhood have always had me seek and create green spaces to the extent possible, and it makes a difference.

Whilst healing from a broken leg and bedridden for a few months, it was the tree, the little squirrel who would come by the window, the feral cat calling and our dogs playing that kept me sane. Being able to communicate through video calls to the elephants was also integral till I could see them face-to-face.

Where are these connections? I'd really invite you to go back in memory and visualise a trip to the forest, or a lake, and just notice how your body shifts.

I can feel my energy expanding while writing about this experience. Rather than saying we're disconnected from nature, we ought to focus on how to reconnect. This will allow us to tap into both the outer and inner animal—our instincts. It's about the primordial oneness we have with nature, being a part of life and nature itself.

Often, I've been told how lucky it is to be with elephants. However, there is really nothing special about me. By giving them respect and listening to what is being communicated in the *field*, and accepting their decision to engage or not. Elephants are part of nature, part of life, and giving them their rightful place and respect is key. Animals, and especially elephants, can see your soul. Truly feel they see your soul.

I feel elephants are so much more evolved than us, and I could be totally biased. But later encountered Jung's talks on the divinity of elephants, which resonated deeply. In the earlier chapters, we discussed African classification. The hierarchy begins with elephants, followed by lions and crocodiles. Humans are placed fourth in this classification. Even if one doesn't want to believe that our consciousness isn't at its highest level, it's important to acknowledge that there may be something more and a reason why other animals exist in our universe.

Everything does not have to be in context with us humans, right?

While travelling to Dharamshala—a hill station, one of the staff members asked me with pure innocence, "What do you get from elephants?" I didn't understand, so he clarified, saying, "Compared to a cow that gives me milk, the elephant doesn't have any utilitarian purpose." It was shocking at first and then exclaimed, "They nourish my soul." Not sure he understood it, though! Imagine if the elephant or the lion asked, "What do we get from humans?" Animals accept the divine order of things and don't go around claiming all land and forests as theirs, the way we humans have been doing!

Giving each other space is very essential. But also, the other question is, do we need to see everything from an anthropomorphic perspective?

I invite you to look at how you can re-engage. How can we reconnect to nature, to the animal, to the animal's soul? It could aid us in rediscovering our own souls. Our very own soul. Yeah, and if you get a chance to look into the eyes of an animal, there's an ocean of love and wisdom. They speak without speaking, and we face ourselves without our masks.

Every time I look at my 'little one—Leela' and into her lovely eyes, I am amazed at the depth of her elephant soul, the wisdom that she carries, and the enormity of her spirit. Also, the love she showers on me—soulful rendezvous indeed!

The hope is to truly reconnect us all to that space of innocence and purity. Their small but deep eyes paint a picture of serenity, a sense of oneness, and invite us to see the larger picture of things.

How small our problems seem when we are amidst an enormous mountain. It feels like being held by Mother Nature and is far more equipped than our small brains. It'll stop overthinking and worrying about the future, which is a bane for mental health.

Have you noticed how much more relaxed people are in the countryside, which is more in sync with natural tides? We can't force the yield to happen faster unless it is by artificial means with obvious repercussions.

To conclude this chapter, I want to emphasise how my innate connection with nature allowed me to anticipate what we would encounter during a Shaman workshop in a natural environment. The messages found their way to me through nature's dance.

When I told the trainers that I sensed and heard peacocks, they didn't believe it till a staff member clarified that the peacocks were just outside my room that morning. That's when I knew that I was reconnecting with my natural instincts. This was also when I began to hold nature in me without being torn apart and looked forward to integrating my worlds in the so-called city!

* * *

Reflections

1. What helps you connect to yourself and the world around you?
2. What's your daily ritual that you enjoy? Make this your me-time.
3. How can you build a morning and night supportive ritual?
4. What brought you joy today?

Notes

1. **Nada Yoga**: A form of yoga that utilises sound vibrations and inner listening to achieve deep meditation and spiritual harmony.

2. **Simone Biles**: An acclaimed American gymnast who withdrew from the Tokyo Olympics in 2021, prioritising her mental health, and sparking discussions on athlete well-being.
3. **Anam Cara**: John O'Donohue's "Anam Cara" is a book with a collection of poems.
4. **Abhisheka**: A Hindu ritual of bathing a deity's idol with sacred substances like milk, water, or honey, symbolising purification and devotion.
5. **Tao**: A concept in Chinese philosophy, signifying the underlying natural order of the universe and emphasising living in harmony with the flow of life.
6. **Dionysian**: Refers to the Greek god Dionysus, representing primal instincts, ecstatic experience, and emotional freedom in opposition to rationality.

Chapter 8

SACRED ELEPHANTS

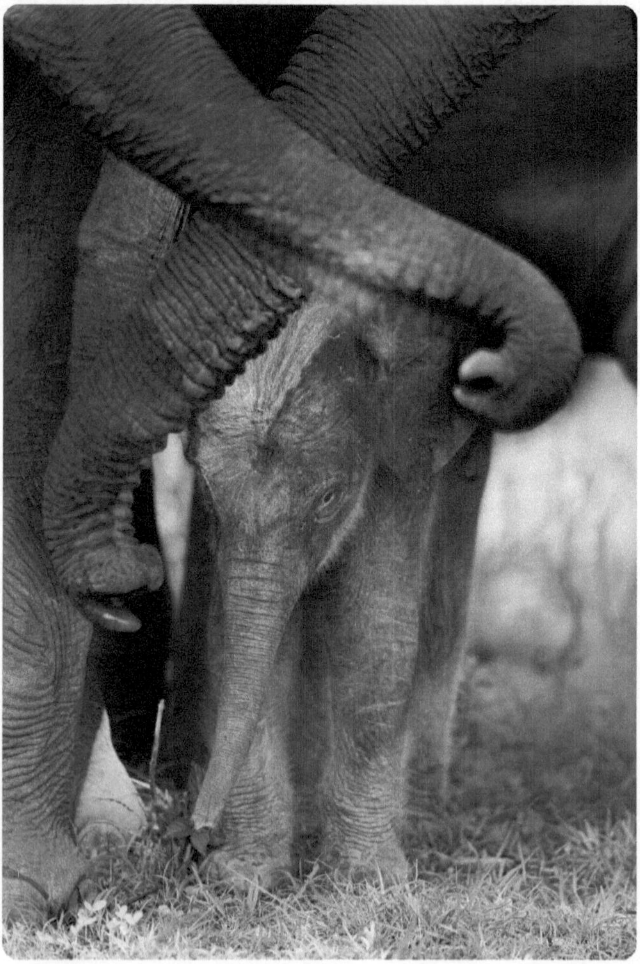

"Mother, I feel you under my feet,
Mother, I hear your heartbeat (x2)
Heya heya heya heya hey oh (x2)"
"Mother, I feel you"- Dianne Martin, 1996

The song beautifully echoes the elephant's intricate connection to Mother Earth.

"Mother, why an elephant?"

Listen, O child, E for elephant, E for Earth. The Elephant listens to my heartbeat through her feet, the seismic vibrations. I know of the planet as she moves, besieging rain with the thumping of her feet, bringing glee to the inhabitants of my planet.

My special child, the greatest masterpiece. But why? What's so special? Elephants are the mega gardeners blooming and helping thrive in the very place they move through. *The ecosystem engineers.* Without them, there are no forests. Forests thrive with the elephants. The trees bow down to the mighty giant, yet they are the gentle beast with ancient ancestry, related to the *manatees*[1].

Elephants possess remarkable swimming skills and exhibit strong camaraderie. They are led by the matriarch, the wisest female elephant, whose knowledge has been passed down through generations. She tactfully guides her herd and teaches them to be in sync with me and nature.

They are also 'water diviners'. But how? They can sense water hidden deep in the earth, through their trunk and as they create these small water pools, many species, including the king of the forest, the lion, the cheetah, the deer and others look forward to this spring of hope.

Elephants are *the keystone species*. Why is that? You'd ask. Because even her dung helps smaller creatures live.

Oh humans, do you know she even helps you by reducing the carbon imprint as she breaks down the small trees, helping the larger ones grow? Besides, elephants mitigate climate change too!

Any surprise, we are in awe of this magical being with the tusk of the crescent moon, the shape of her ear, akin to the place she lives upon,

Asia or Africa. She moves, as guided by her spatial ancient memory. Indeed, you cannot stop her.

Elephants are doing their divine duty, to enliven, to build, to shift the energy of the place, of the planet, and our earth. What will you choose, my child? E for elephants or E for extinction and bring about the extinction of us all.

Yes mother, I would very much want to say E for elephants, *Aane²*. I hope many, many generations will be able to share the wonder of these magical beings in their lives.

May we cherish the gentle giants who grace our lives.

Web of Life

Firstly, this section will address and delve into 'sacred ecology'.

Let's begin by understanding *ecology*. To be honest, I initially thought it had to do with nature. Over time, it dawned on me that it's the *interconnectedness*, or the relationship between the unique elements of species in nature, including humans (yes, we are also one species of nature) on planet Earth and the environment, per se.

Interestingly, the vet at the sanctuary shared her insights on a podcast on interconnectedness. The speaker expresses her relation with nature, beginning with happier times when she'd go into the forest, and would hear music and sounds of nature. Gradually, the forest became quieter and quieter, mainly because the land is shrinking and degraded. The forest was going silent and perhaps grieving the loss, as the podcaster was tuned into the soul of the land.

At one of the first shaman workshops, I conveyed a strong sense of detachment from Bengaluru, mainly because the Garden City was no longer green. Hence, desired to escape from the city, primarily, to be surrounded by nature. Then, I learnt about the 'spirit' of a place, which intrigued me.

It is crucial to tune into the energy of the place, whether it is our birthplace or the place we now call home. This is reminiscent of the deep connection I had with my maternal grandparents, even though they have passed away. Their memories keep the spirit alive within me. I will forever carry a piece of the Malnad region within my being.

Unfortunately, Malnad itself is undergoing drastic changes, with green spaces disappearing at an alarming rate.

What comes into your reverie now? Any memories? What and where do you perceive a connection with?

I would like to narrate an incident wherein we were driving down to Sakleshpur, a hilly region in Karnataka. We were enthusiastic, but suddenly our energy level dropped. As we crossed a patch of broken trees. I understood that we sensed the pain of the region, the trees and the landscape. Our shaman trainer guided us to send prayer and healing energy to the place.

Similar to what I also feel with the elephants—their pain and anguish. We know a little of their stories, but we don't have the entirety of their history.

How much have we broken down Mother Earth!

Stephen Aizenstat, founder of 'Dream Tending' elucidates that the dreamscape could also be communicating about the land and nature. May we be in reverence as the space is communing with us, literally talking to us.

The reason it was apt to bring this is to see things in their entirety—the larger web of life, which we are part of—humans and elephants!

In this chapter, we will discuss elephants and their ethology, including their behaviour. Through reading and discussions with conservationists, I've grown to understand the necessity of a holistic approach to these issues.

Capturing and Recapture of Arikomban

Let us begin with *Arikomban*[3]—known as the rice-eating tusker. Many complaints arose as he approached the rice storage areas near human settlements. As a result, he was captured and relocated to a different location. However, despite efforts, he continued to wander back, leading to subsequent recaptures and relocations. This raised concerns among animal advocates, who protested against what they perceived as an unfair situation.

I am going to provide an example to set the context here. Consider the hypothetical scenario where Arikomban is a human. Please forgive me, but I believe it is important at times to make parallels with humans in order to understand that every being has feelings and certain rights, not just us homo sapiens!

Now, let's explore the potential outcome if a child who has been raised in a particular family is suddenly relocated to a different place. To illustrate this, let's reflect on the movie Karate Kid, where the protagonist moves from the U.S. to China, experiencing a profound cultural shock and facing adversity from teenagers. However, he eventually finds solace and support in the character portrayed by Jackie Chan.

Imagine a child you knew, perhaps a bit of a mischief monger, placed in a totally new situation. How would that work? It's neither fair nor right, isn't it?

Now, try to imagine how the elephants must feel in the face of such wrath. This can lead to a sense of frustration and create even more problems.

Conservationists insist just translocating does not help but may cause more issues. They emphasise the need to mitigate conflict through well-planned, scientific procedures.

Importantly, we need to acknowledge the shrinking habitat and, more significantly, realise that elephants have a home range. It is the extent and location of the area covered annually. However, this is influenced by habitat fragmentation, which might lead to traverse to other areas, especially in search of water and food, thereby leading to potential conflict with humans.

At an elephant event, I heard a touching story. A gentleman shared that a herd passing through his farm stayed back for one or two days because one of the calves passed away. The herd didn't do any damage, though. In honour of the calf, he built a small cemetery. His words, "Every year, around the same time, the herd comes to pay homage where the little calf rests," are deeply moving.

One wonders on this inner knowing that they sense that I have shared about our elephants as well.

Do we recognise their wisdom?

The largest land mammals, elephants, have brains that are three times bigger than ours and boast three times more nerve cells. Their memory is truly immense. It begs the question: what makes us believe that we alone possess feelings and have the ability to do anything and everything, even at the expense of nature, in this case predominantly elephants?

"They say an elephant never forgets. What they don't tell you is, you never forget an elephant."

— **Bill Murray**

As for Arikomban, the continuous capturing attempts failed to resolve the issue initially, and it was reported to have settled down at the KMTR reserve. They even moved him to two different places. This relocation, at times, created significant problems.

But what happens when we're totally moved into a new place without warning and context?

Arikomban must have felt abandoned in such circumstances. It's possible that he had a tribe of elephants he was connected to, and he may have even grown accustomed to a specific habitat.

While it is important to prioritise the safety of both humans and elephants, one cannot help but question if captures are the only solution. Just a few days ago, one of the mahouts was discussing a capture in Karnataka and shared a perspective. He related it to a blind elephant that I had also encountered at a camp. Thankfully, this elephant was saved after being shot in both eyes by farmers while entering a private farm. The mahout expressed worry about last year's loss of numerous wild elephants, mentioning that capture can help save them, especially in such cases. I too wonder about the path ahead.

There is a problem, and not the individual (human or elephant)—the circumstances itself.

I am sitting with, what is the problem? We need to consider the ecosystem for an effective solution.

The moment an elephant engages in any of these behaviours, such as Arikomban, similar incidents continue to occur, even if no harm is done. Despite the complexity of the situation, they're categorised as rogue animals.

In another context, while working with one of the kabaddi leagues, there was a key player who was considered a problem, and I was advised not to meet him. I insisted and sought his support to improve the team's performance rather than ignoring him. After our discussion, during a practice session, he loudly greeted me with *"namaste doctorji"* (hello doctor) from across the room, surprising many in the management. My stance was simple: to address the problem at hand and treat him with respect as a senior player. Building that connection and reintegrating him into the team was crucial. From *"mujhme koi problem nahi hai"* (I don't have any problem) to *"yeh team problem ka kya kare mam"* (how shall we work on this team issue?) was a monumental shift. In fact, he helped in getting to the root cause of the management's struggle with handling losses. As expected, the team started winning from the next season. To reinstate, there was indeed a problem, but the player himself was not the problem.

More recently, it was a case of smart, compassionate thinking by the main in-charge of the railway line, in northeastern states, including Assam and West Bengal. Through the AI-based system, he spotted a large herd of around 60 elephants. The loco pilot urged the driver to apply the emergency brakes and prevented the accident.

Thankfully, this saved all the elephants and averted an enormous tragedy—the herd from breaking and facing death because of his vigilance.

However, it raises an important question: how many people will follow suit and show empathy towards these majestic creatures?

A poignant social media post caught my attention. Let us imagine an elephant crossing the road. Now read the message below: **"The elephant is not crossing the road; the road is crossing the forest."**

How many forests have we sacrificed, especially for the sake of growth, including the railway lines?

How aware are we of what is happening?

At our World Elephant Day celebration on August 10 '2024, conservationist Vinod Krishnan elucidated the concept of space and its importance, to be aware and take responsibility for what's happening around us. He stated, *"Space is important for us, but also for a lot of other beings, especially elephants. These animals require vast territories to survive. Ultimately, it is up to us to share our world with them and respect their space. Elephants require vast spaces to roam and thrive. Understanding their needs and respecting their natural behaviour is crucial for their survival."*

We have fragmented crucial elephant corridors and pathways in the name of development. Railway lines, dams and other infrastructure projects are being built, which are hampering animal movement. However, the elephant, with its ancient memory transmitted across generations, still holds onto its earlier spatial memory. As a result, it continues to traverse the same paths and crosses railway tracks, leading to tragic railway deaths.

The restoration of elephant corridors is ongoing, thanks to the tireless efforts of organisations, including the Wildlife Trust of India and A Rocha, supporting the Forest Department.

More such developments are being witnessed in our own Bannerghatta landscape, as stated by Avinash Krishnan, Director of A Rocha. He shared the following message for this book: "My dedication to elephant conservation stands as a beacon of hope, blending science, compassion and action to ensure these mega mammals thrive for generations to come. The least amount of land area is what we need to protect in order for elephants to roam freely, as elephant corridors are the lifelines of co-existence, fostering harmony between wildlife and humanity. Our pledge is to support the protection of elephant corridors in the Bannerghatta-Hosur landscape."

Respect

Some say elephants are known to be introverts, and even if they are not, we've impinged on their space.

Even during safaris, our main goal is to have fun. It's breathtaking to be surrounded by elephants and spot other animals. However, is it necessary for us to keep disturbing their terrain??

One of our professors used to scold students when he caught them mindlessly plucking leaves, reminding them that "it hurts them."

A cousin in Malnad once reprimanded us for throwing pebbles into the lake, telling us, "You wouldn't throw stones at your mother (water)." I am grateful for these lessons and teachings received early in life, perhaps forging the way for the deep relationships with nature and animals.

I chanced upon a video from a camp that allows for distant observation and interaction. Kids were making fun and screaming loudly at an elephant. He was a young bull and began chasing them away- swinging his trunk and mock charging. His actions were not aggressive, rather an attempt to get them out of sight. There was a clear barricade in place to ensure safety and distance. Either the parent or mahout gently remarked, "you are troubling him and hence he's behaving in that manner". I have experienced similar situations in camps, where the mahout's advice is often disregarded, much to their frustration. The video was a lovely message, to instil empathy and the right action if taken into consideration.

Remember when I first started interacting with Leela? I approached her gently from a distance and asked, "Are you Leela?". We keep discussing this even in sanctuary spaces that not all elephants are inherently social, and would want to connect to every other being, whether human or elephants. It is perfectly fine and essential to give them the respect and space they require.

'Respect'—it really boils down to respect.

Just think about how we want to be treated.

This concept applies not only to elephants but even to your house animals, or your companions, or what many people call pets.

Can we remember this aspect of space, and what we understand, especially with the elephant species' behaviour. They need a lot of space to be an Elephant!

At the sanctuary, a new elephant was just about settling. We were interacting outside her shed. She shoved her trunk, meaning 'move away.' She was very clear that, "No, I don't want you all here now." We ought to give animals time and space to gradually accept with trust and care, and not sheer control through dominance.

Human Need to Overpower and Establish Dominance

We need to examine why we seek to be entertained constantly by other species, which seems to be a hallmark of our species alone! Are we so bored or disconnected from ourselves and life that we seek it outside, and does it satiate us?

Why is domination necessary? It struck me deeply.

I have observed that this phenomenon occurs with certain mahouts as well. There was one particular case where a mahout was able to initially handle a difficult elephant. As time went on, he would proudly proclaim, "Oh, she listens to me." However, I couldn't sense a genuine connection or understanding between them.

My impression was that he was a little inflated since he only communicated using commands. He wouldn't read and interpret what was happening to the elephant. However, when she got triggered, he couldn't effectively control or rather calm her. His only impression was coming from, "She listens to me." Simply put, what is the concept of listening in their context? No matter what, she should follow my commands.

Even with Leela, when I am with her, she doesn't listen to the mahouts. Thankfully, her current mahout, and everyone around, understand that she just wants to be with me. Her mahout jokingly says, "You are her clutch, accelerator and brake."

It's like one of the young elite athletes who has experienced a lot of ups and downs. As soon as she sees me (we mostly have online sessions), she exclaims, "The minute I see you, I feel things are fine." Now she's just beginning to spread her wings and embark on life's journey.

It seems like a proud mother moment!

Now, we need to ask ourselves, when and why do I need to overpower?

What's the message here? What's the opportunity that's being conveyed? When I am overpowering, I am superficially inflated, and what is it compensating for?

It's vital to look at, as humans, because we need to come together as a race to sustain ourselves, if not anything else. How can we be oblivious to the sheer amount of climate change happening around the world? As I write this chapter, a few weeks back, the 'Elephant Nature Park' in Thailand had severe flooding, and they lost two-three elephants. Just when these captive elephants, who got a second chance, face this tragic end, even then, you wonder, what was their message?

Kusha's longing to be Free, and Stay Connected to Mahouts

The story of elephant Kusha from the *Dubare* Elephant camp in Coorg, Karnataka, comes to mind. He was captured because a few elephants were causing trouble in the plantation region and were brought to Dubare. He got accustomed to the camp with good caretakers looking after him. However, he eventually wandered away, apparently in search of a mate. The caretakers and management were worried, searched and brought him back to the camp. But he wandered away again, driven by his innate instinct. Surprisingly, he returned with two females and another male.

There was a statement in the paper that said, "We've taken care so well that he returns to the camp. But we need to follow the government's order to be released." They mentioned that he still roams around Dubare.

It's okay to roam around as long as he's not lost his natural ability to live in the wild, which is unfortunately common among captive elephants. As caretakers, we want what is best for them, but we also want to provide the choice to live freely. Kusha seems to have the best of both worlds. But sadly, the same cannot be said for many other elephants who have lost their freedom. Kusha's case bears resemblance to the Sheldrick Trust's rewilding initiative, which focuses on rehabilitating orphaned elephants in Kenya.

Rivaldo says, 'Not again humans – you broke my trust.'

Finally, I would like to discuss the case of Rivaldo. Once again, his capture should not have taken place.

He had become accustomed to feeding from humans. Exactly why it is essential to maintain a distance between especially the wild, and the public. Thankfully, he was released back into the wild. As per the sources, he no longer relied on humans for sustenance, which is a positive outcome. Synchronously, as I was thinking about Rivaldo, a post from a conservationist's friend appeared, as if Rivaldo was guiding the chapter too!

But we must not forget the tragic incident of the *pineapple bomb* (pineapple containing firecrackers/explosives inside) in Kerala, where an elephant consumed it, and sadly died after suffering immensely. Sources from the region said it was for pests, not elephants.

This elephant was also heavily pregnant, which made the situation even more distressing. It was deeply disturbing when I received pictures of the pregnant elephant and the unborn calf.

Is this our humanity?

There are many aspects to this issue, though. It makes me wonder how low humanity would shrink. That is the question that arises. Despite knowing that we need the elephants, if not for them, for our own selfish self.

As mentioned before, they're the ecosystem engineers, as forests thrive because of them. Mega gardeners, as their dung help other species. They aid in forest growth, creating a conducive environment for other species to live. Most importantly, they also have a positive impact from a human perspective by reducing carbon emissions. As they move, they selectively remove smaller trees, allowing larger trees to grow and absorb more carbon dioxide.

When will the importance of this species dawn on us, along with the myths we have discussed, especially those involving Airavata and water itself? Elephants are often referred to as water diviners, as they possess an innate knowledge of where to find water sources and how to access them. During the peak of summer, when water is scarce, other animals rely on elephants for their survival as they create water pools.

African research has also shown that elephants clearly distinguish who means well to them—the intent. For instance, if it's a tribe that supports and cares for them, they're relaxed. But if it's a tribe that hunts them, their stress level goes up by merely listening to the voice.

From a Jungian lens, we look at things from a curious and analytical approach. We should be reflecting on the need to overpower and exert control.

Changing Landscapes

When it comes to elephants, people have diverse reactions and emotions. For those who work closely with them, such as the mahouts, there is a mix of awe and fear. This holds true for the general population as well.

What does the presence of elephants evoke in you now? What about nature as a whole? Particularly, in recent times, when we have witnessed the relentless fury of nature. If we continue on our current trajectory without adequately protecting our elephants, we will only bring about more destruction to our planet and ourselves.

The occurrence of extreme climate is being witnessed worldwide at an alarming rate, with the current example being the wildfires in California, United States. Sometimes it makes me wonder what this means for our future.

So, to look at *what in me is malnourished, what in me is captive, that I get a high in overpowering the elephants, the largest land mammals?*

It is crucial to pay attention to this, because when we block space or it is impinged, it creates stress, frustration, irritation—be it for humans or other animals.

Imagine with key elephant corridors being fragmented, ancient pathways being used or taken away from the elephants. This is deeply affecting them. It's causing more stress. It affects communication between herds and then it shouldn't be a surprise that they strike back. They're claiming what used to be their space.

If a stranger comes into your house, are you going to keep muted? I believe this metaphor holds true. No matter how many barricades or obstacles we put in their way, conservationists say that elephants are smart enough to find a way around them. It reminds me of how we manoeuvre traffic jams to get to our destination.

Why should we assume that other species lack the same motivation or skills? One crucial aspect of the solution is to acknowledge the natural behaviour of these species and understand that our overconsumption and expansion have perhaps heightened conflicts or negative interactions between humans and elephants. It's unfair to blame only the elephants; the loss of forests and fragmented forests are a major factor.

Play—Crucial for Well-being

At this juncture, I would like to introduce the concept of 'play', which is used in therapy as well. When a client engages in play, as detailed in the Leela chapter, it signifies that the person is settling into their comfort zone.

With elephants, it is through mud baths, mud pools and playful interactions among themselves—curious and exploring. The young also engage in mock fights or sparring matches.

But, when their space is impeached, it might lead to stress. Can one still play?

Play is essential, not just for humans, but for elephants as well. Imagine the stress and absence of play in captivity, and being separated from their herd.

Do we want to see them play? We need to think about that.

The immense joy I felt when Leela first started playing can't be put into words. Over time, she began playing with others. The other elephants reaching out to engage with her is heartening.

Can we be the species that we're supposed to be and open ourselves to give these beautiful beings a true chance at life, thereby making our own lives meaningful?

As the book draws to a close, I believe our hope for salvation rests on rectifying the consequences—intended or otherwise—of our past generations' actions in their drive for advancement.

Gajanana and Lobhasura—Demon of Greed

Finally, tying up this chapter with *Gajanana*[4], who is the fourth *avatar*[5] of Lord Ganesha, and was called upon to destroy *Lobhasura*[6]. *Lobha* translates to 'greed', and it's considered the demon. One of our own 'vices.'

The story goes like this: *Kubera*[7] is smitten by the Goddess in Kailash, and as a result, Asura (demon) is born. Ardently praying, he obtains Shiva's boon and becomes invincible. As expected, he becomes a menace and aims to destroy all the gods.

In response, the oppressed gods, also known as the devas (virtues), call upon Gajanana. The demon's consciousness is evoked and upon realising his wrongdoing, he attains salvation through Gajanana.

What is our greed? We all experience it for certain things. In my case, it is greed for books. It could be different things for different people. For instance, when emotions are running berserk, many of us may tend to overwork, binge-watch Netflix or use food as a distraction.

Understanding this aspect is of paramount importance. It's okay to dissociate or disconnect at times, but challenges can still persist in your mind unnoticed, masked by distractions like scrolling or binge-watching. Self-awareness is the key.

I am shocked at how empty our human race seems to be, that we rely so heavily on external stimulation. We are constantly busy doing and expanding, but at what cost?

The vice that we need to watch and call upon to support is Gajanana, our inner Gajanana. Whether or not you're religious, we could seek the archetype to help us deal with this greed. Through this, we could wholeheartedly celebrate nature, cherish every being and the gentle beasts.

Elephants can be observed from a distance, experiencing a sense of joy and contentment similar to the robotic elephants we are seeing. This way, we can protect the real ones.

As we conclude, let us remember and recite the *Shanti mantra*[9]— *Om Shanti Shanti Shanti* which signifies peace to the two-legged beings, the four-legged beings and the entire cosmos.

***

Reflections

1. What does sacred mean to you?
2. How do we cherish elephants naturally?
3. When do I feel overpowered or overpower another?
4. Build a sacred ritual to help connect to nature, elephants, and life.

Notes

1. **Manatees**: Large aquatic mammals known as "sea cows," distantly related to elephants. They symbolise the interconnectedness of all life and are a reminder of the need for the conservation of vulnerable species.
2. **Aane**: The Kannada word for "elephant," emphasising the cultural and linguistic diversity in the reverence for elephants in India, particularly in South Indian traditions.
3. **Arikomban**: A famous wild tusker from Kerala, India, The name translates to "rice-eating tusker," highlighting the complex human-elephant conflict and the need for co-existence strategies.
4. **Gajanana**: A Sanskrit term meaning "elephant-faced one," referring to Lord Ganesha.
5. **Avatar**: A Sanskrit term meaning "incarnation" or "descent," used to describe divine beings manifesting on Earth. The term can metaphorically link elephants to their divine, sacred roles in the ecosystem and human imagination.

6. **Lobhasura**: A mythological demon symbolising greed, derived from "lobha," the Sanskrit word for greed.
7. **Kubera**: The Hindu god of wealth and prosperity.
8. **Mukti**: A Sanskrit term meaning liberation or spiritual freedom.
9. **Shanti mantra**: A Vedic chant for peace, harmony, and well-being. The term reflects the need for inner and outer peace.

Chapter 9

ANIMA MUNDI ~ THE WORLD SOUL BECKONS

"But perhaps the most important lesson I learned is that there are no walls between humans and the elephants except those that we put up ourselves and that until we allow not only elephants but all living creatures their place in the sun, we can never be whole ourselves."
– Lawrence Anthony, Elephant Whisperer

"*Gajalakshmi*—the mother of elephants reveals her cosmic glory. The feminine emerging gracefully from the ocean with the elephants as her constant companions. This powerful depiction has been lingering all along in the collective unconscious, waiting patiently until we are ready to embrace it.

Akshobhya, the blue *Buddha* along with his *vajra* (diamond) the elephant, made its way to my consciousness gradually.

In a gentle nudge from the nurturing goddess and benevolent Buddha, I was reminded to embrace the divine elephants and my own higher consciousness.

The cosmic mystery unfolds in both our micro and macro universes."—CS.

Anima Mundi is in my space whilst gearing up for this final chapter. Upon awakening, a sudden burst of insight flooded my mind, reminding me of the artefact that had caught my attention during a Jungian dream retreat in Palakkad, Kerala. I've not been one for chokers or extravagant jewellery, but this particular necklace, adorned with both elephants and peacocks, spoke to me. Synchronously, it called out to me just as elephants had entered my life, during a transformative dream retreat surrounded by breathtaking nature.

The dance between my inner and outer worlds was in perfect synchrony, and my psyche was open to the mysterious wonders.

The mother of elephants—the Elephant Goddess, Gajalakshmi has held me during that challenging phase. It was only later that I realised her feminine essence as a holding symbol. However, she had always been present in the collective consciousness, waiting to be welcomed. Finally, the divine feminine, the embodiment of the great mother energy, is now beginning to awaken in our consciousness.

What do elephants mean to me, and to many others in various forms? What message does this totem convey? Let us delve into the legend to find out.

Gajalakshmi and Her Nature Beings

We draw much inspiration from legends and stories. Therefore, it is appropriate to introduce the energy of the Goddess at this juncture. The churning of the ocean, which is described in the Palakapya chapter, is closely related to the Airavata. It is also associated with the Goddess as she disappears into the ocean, awaiting our awakening. According to sources, she is said to have emerged with elephants from the deep waters after eons of churning by the devas and asuras (god and demons) for the elixir.

The legend implies that in this age, we have become a "doing society". Thereby shunning away the feminine, which then requires us to begin an inward journey to reclaim and connect to the feminine—akin to the path of individuation (living our unique destiny). The ocean really is a significant symbol of taking the journey—going into the depths, encountering the shadow—the poison and holding it all to see what emerges as the elixir. Hence, the goddess signifies alchemy—'inner gold' as depicted in her images.

In hindsight, Leela's story is akin to the legend, or a figment of my imagination. Witnessing her transformation from a distressed elephant to a gentle spirit has been heartwarming. She really was deep in the ocean. So, what seemed like a rescue to others was swimming in the deep waters for her. Leela had to be freed from the old system, which was a ***concretisation of the symbol into a sign,*** and even worse, holding the elephant, or so-called God, in captivity.

As I was wondering about the lure towards this legend and the sacred images one encounters in temple architecture and heritage sites, it slowly dawned that this is perhaps the journey of modern women and society, to reclaim our divine feminine and the alchemical gold that emerges after plunging into the depths of the ocean!

As mentioned in previous chapters, the Elephant Spirit appeared in my dreams, preparing me for the physical encounter. Because when I met these majestic beings, floodgates of emotions opened, and I had to touch my own vulnerability and depth.

It was a profoundly mystical experience, and I am still in awe of being of service to these gentle giants.

It is a reminder that when human society becomes disconnected from 'numinous nature' and disregards the feminine; the goddess retreats into the depths of the ocean. She patiently waits until we embark on the sea voyage, which may seem like an unjust detour or curse. Carl Jung lamented this loss of connection with the oneness.

*"The development of Western philosophy during the last two centuries has succeeded in isolating the mind in its own sphere and in severing it from its **primordial oneness with the universe**. Man himself has ceased to be the microcosm and eidolon of the cosmos, and his 'Anima' is no longer the consubstantial scintilla, spark of the Anima Mundi, World Soul"* (CW 11, par. 759).

In another version, Gajendra—a devotee of Vishnu, though being a king in an earlier birth was cursed to be born an elephant by a sage. Yet, he remained an ardent devotee worshipping Vishnu. His daily ritual included circumambulating (pradakshina) his God, and so would Goddess Lakshmi. The Goddess, however, was quicker. When Vishnu sees that Gajendra wished to be the first to worship him, he suggests that Lakshmi be seated beside him.

Gajendra realises the benevolent gesture and initially worships them both. Then, he swiftly runs to a riverbank; fills his trunk with water, and performs the abhisheka—spraying water on the Goddess to express his gratitude. The Goddess is surprised and gleeful at this loving gesture by Gajendra. The gods who witness this blissful scene then bestow Lakshmi, the name of *Gajalakshmi, the Lakshmi of elephants,* the mother of elephants who takes care of her benevolent beings.

It'll be wonderful if we could hold both, the mother, the Great Mother archetype, who nurtures her beings, and the Divine Mother who emerges from the depths after being besieged by the world. This is perhaps why we are drawn to the wisdom of the elephants, an ancient memory of the oceanic depths and our inner understanding, as reflected in our cultural legends.

Aane Habba—Celebration of Elephants

Aane Habba, also known as the Elephant Festival, is a celebration of that relationship that symbolises the nurturing of Mother Nature. This is a nature-based festival where the festivities last for three days and involve the worship of the Goddess Gajalakshmi, alongside clay elephant sculptures. These sculptures are either immersed in water or left beneath a banyan tree, similar to the Ganesha visarjan ritual. This gesture is symbolic of celebrating the elephants, for what they truly are and where they belong, amidst nature—free and wild.

If we reflect and go back to the necklace or the artefact, it calls out to me. What does it suggest? Has this happened to you before? Perhaps it evokes a certain energy or another totem for you.

In the same way, the feminine symbolises the womb and the depths of existence, just like the majestic elephants with their wisdom and grandeur. It is difficult to put into words the sense of awe that this brings.

I was thrilled when Manasa.K.S., our head Jungian trainer, sent me wishes for the Aane Habba festival with clay elephant images. Synchronously, this was before the Symbolism talk titled 'Trumpeting the emergence of the divine elephant'. The Goddess seemed to have made her way into the talk and my heart.

During preparation for the talk, as I tuned into the elephantine energy, the trunk emerged as a symbol of love. However, I don't mean romantic love alone. It represents an all-encompassing love that holds the 'other' with awe and compassion, rather than reacting solely out of fear.

I invite you to take a moment to turn inward. What are you sitting with? Explore your own emotions, feelings, and associations.

The World Soul

"The Anima Mundi, the world soul, is the presence of 'Spirit' within matter. The world soul grows plants and animates animals, giving us vitality, creativity and the capacity to fulfil our desires."

– Carl Jung

The world soul, or world psyche, is referred to as the Anima Mundi. Sri Aurobindo echoes Jung's sentiment, *"Hidden nature is secret God"*.

It is intriguing to consider why and how we have lost this connection, which was once a crucial aspect of our ancestors.

Stephen Harding, in his book Animate Earth, recommends Gaian science to help us reconnect to Anima Mundi and go beyond the human-centric worldview (2017). We must find our way back home to nature, reconnecting with any aspect that draws us in.

In my personal experience, it is connected to elephants, which stems from the natural richness and simplicity of my childhood in Malnad, a society deeply rooted in nature. There, nature worship, such as *Gange Pooje* (River Goddess) and *Bhoomi Hunime* (Gaia/Earth), was an integral part of our festivities. It makes me wonder if elephants, with their ability to truly see beyond the exterior, sense this connection to the 'Oneness' of the world and our souls.

Now, let's delve deeper into the concept of Anima Mundi, or the world soul, also known as the *unus-mundus*. This idea aligns with Jung's concept of the collective unconscious and Rupert Sheldrake's theory of morphic resonance. To me, Anima Mundi represents a unified field where our intentions align with our actions, allowing us to become one with it and be guided.

More Than Human World—David Abram

Interestingly, I happened to come across articles about human-animal transformation from the perspectives of Native Americans, similar to our own indigenous societies. These discuss the concept of interconnectedness and how we influence each other. The more I reflect on this, the more I agree, especially when I think about my experiences with Leela and our other elephants.

Psyche encompasses not only the individual human but also other beings and species, particularly elephants, in my case. David Abram, an ecologist and philosopher, speaks of the 'more than human world,' which deeply resonates with me.

Jeanne Lacourt, Jungian Analyst from a native indigenous society, succinctly explains what I feel about the elephants. They sensed a connection, much like what my dreams were trying to convey, by tapping into the energy field. Leela drew me in and together we entered a shared connected field, with others observing from the sidelines. Her attention primarily revolves around me, gradually including others. This is precisely why I say, when asked if I work with elephants, "I am not sure who works on whom".

I perceive a relational field where we recalibrate and co-create. This, to me, is the field of potential, a gift from nature's gentle giants.

In fact, our energies synchronise because I do not feel small, and they do not seem big or act in a way that makes them bigger. For that matter, it's the resonance in your energy that determines the field.

During my PhD years in Australia, I had a soulful rendezvous with dolphins which lasted 4 years. As I observed them by the river, I felt a sense of connection and wondered if we were silently communicating. On the final day, they gracefully danced close to the shore as I bid farewell to the river that had supported my journey during those years in Perth. Although I never swam with them, we shared a profound connection from our separate spaces.

Tara—The Wise Elephant Senses Her Ancestors

Tara, the elephant that guided and inspired Mark Shand to become a conservationist, serves as an excellent example to illustrate the field. In his account of their remarkable journey across India, Shand (1991) recounts a noteworthy incident that took place in Dhauli, Odisha. This location was the site of one of history's bloodiest wars, so intense that the river supposedly turned red.

Upon entering the place, the group could feel the palpable dense energy, but it was Tara who was most affected. She grew cautious and agitated. The Kalinga War had claimed the lives of countless animals, including elephants and horses. Despite the mahout's efforts to coax her, Tara adamantly refused to enter the site. Perhaps she sensed the presence of her ancestors. Elephants are known to mourn and show respect when they encounter the remnants of their ancestors who are ancient beings. This moving story exemplifies the depth of their being.

Morphic Resonance and Group Soul

Pertaining to the lines by Lawrence Anthony, mentioned at the start of this chapter, echoes my sentiments about the world soul and the wholeness of our being. Normally, when I visit Leela, she eagerly waits for me by the gate, almost as if she somehow knows, being attuned to the *field*, that I am about to arrive.

In relation to this topic, Rupert Sheldrake, an author and parapsychology researcher, argues that 'morphic resonance' is similar to the field we have been discussing. He believes animals possess a group soul and are capable of sensing the happenings in distant locations. Elephants, for instance, are known for their inherent wisdom and likely have an awareness of what is happening to the species across different regions as well as by being attuned to the Earth.

The relationship between dogs and their human companions offers a good example of morphic resonance. Sheldrake conducted experiments to explore the ability of dogs to detect their human companion's return. The studies revealed that dogs exhibit anticipatory behaviour, like waiting by the door or window, even in situations where the timing is uncertain and the mode of transportation is unfamiliar. These findings imply that dogs may have a connection to a morphic field that connects them to their human companions, allowing them to perceive when their owner is en route home. I am sure this is a phenomenon that has intrigued us about our dog companions. Caesar—our dog would ensure the front door was open when me and my sister returned from school or work!

Shiva and Bunti—Forest Man and Elephant in the Forest

Byju's book titled 'Matriarch, Autobiography of an Elephant (2022)' weaves a strong narrative. It tells the story of Shiva, a forest man, and the journey of a young elephant. They are connected yet respectfully distant, respecting the space for the species, unless it's absolutely necessary, mainly to help the elephants.

The book encapsulates the changes in the landscape, the shrinking habitat, the increasing noise caused by vehicles, as well as the adaptations, captures, moments of joy, and losses.

Shiva goes on to become a forest guard aiding conservation, thanks to his reverence for the land and deep bond with the species. A moving narrative of the shift in the terrain that impacts both the human and the animal, and perhaps even their relationship. An insightful book that describes the changing elephant landscape through the eyes of an elephant.

Elephants Show Trust in Humans

I came across the remarkable story written by conservationist Priya Davedar and her husband Jean Puriyawad (2015) about their harmonious existence with elephants in the forest. It truly touched my heart. The conservationists involved displayed a delicate balance of enabling the elephants while also maintaining a respectful distance, intervening only when absolutely necessary. A single instance showcased how elephants sought help because of their trust in them—a bond that was developed over time.

My uncle has a farm in the Bannerghatta region, and shared instances of elephants expressing their dissatisfaction by breaking things around when they required water, for example. It was only when there was a scarcity or insufficiency of water that these magnificent creatures would communicate their distress and needs. In psychology, we look at 'what is the need being communicated' by such acts and behaviours. I often use the phrase 'story behind the story' to uncover the intended meaning. A video of a hungry elephant breaking into a house is making rounds, along with the petrified family.

What I am trying to express is that co-existence is indeed possible, but it has its challenges. It is important to remember that just because we are unaware of something does not mean it does not exist.

Movies like *Kantara, Gandhada Gudi and Avatar* are inspiring examples of films that echo nature and its inhabitants. "Inspiring storytelling is the way to reach masses, and striking a chord to propel conservation efforts." —Emphasised Amogha Varsha, at an Environment Conclave.

I have a favourite story to share about a wonderful person we call Ajji (granny), whom we met at the fruit-picking location. When we first met, I casually mentioned that the fruits were for elephants. Initially, she didn't believe me. Then, what she narrated convinced me that elephants, life and synchronicities guide us, much like a dream knowing its dreamer.

Ajji shared that she hails from Bannerghatta, a place in Bengaluru, where it was customary to worship elephants through their footprints. She believes that her family has never been harmed because of their faith in elephants. They would also offer food as an offering, and their farm has remained untouched. Such beliefs are also echoed by traditional mahout communities. Every time we meet, Ajji gives me a packet full of fruits and says, "This is for my Lakshmi—Gods—the Elephants."

Are these lessons and guidance meant for us? These are thoughts that we should contemplate.

Kuvempu, an Indian writer, believed that nature is divine and that we are all born as *'Vishwamanava'* or universal man. He highlighted that all children are born with this universal nature, but it is the conditioning in life that makes us forget our essence. The goal is to return to our original, pristine state. I would add to the trunk full of love.

Gay Bradshaw (2005) emphasises that at the Sheldrick Centre in Kenya, human caretakers act as allomothers for orphaned elephants, and later rewild them to their natural, wild existence. Bradshaw provides instances of how trauma can affect elephants, even while they are still in the womb, akin to humans. Her groundbreaking work is referred to as trans-species psychology. As I understand more of this concept, I realise it aligns with what I have been doing with elephants. It's something I hadn't recognised before! However, I look at it as being guided and attuned to the field.

Animal Mind

"What happens to the beasts will happen to the man. All things are connected. If the great beasts are gone, man would surely die of a great loneliness of spirit."
—**Chief Seattle of the Nez Perce, 1884.**

In the Kannada (Indian language) movie *Gaalipata*, actor Anant Nag portrays the character of an avid hunter. During hunting, he becomes injured and confined to a wheelchair by a wild boar. After two years, he makes a final attempt to hunt down the boar but finds himself stranded without a gun or companions. The boar, however, spares his life. During the process, he gets back on his feet and, even though an opportunity arises, he refuses to kill the boar. In a moment of awakening, he realises that it was Lord Vishnu in *a varaha avatar*—'form of a bear' that brought his life back akin to an initiation in shamanism.

In Karnataka, there was a notorious smuggler named Veerappan, who dealt in ivory and sandalwood. In a case of mistaken identity, he kidnaps two wildlife filmmakers and holds them captive for two weeks.

They later published a detailed account of their abduction, including an intriguing chapter titled 'Veerappan gapes at the Sacred Elephant'. In this chapter, the filmmakers describe that they witnessed a different side of Veerappan, as he showed admiration towards the elephants and expressed anguish over their current situation.

They even speculate whether he was playing psychological games with their minds. Perhaps the elephants touched Veerappan's soul after living in the same shared space in the jungle.

On a different note, to think of the lives of the marginalised individuals and what makes a person a bandit!

Sacred Elephants

"First worshipped, then sacrificed"
 –Heathcote Williams (1989)

The book, Sacred Elephants, traces how our reverence for elephants turned into control and the inflated need to overpower through horrific practices such as trophy hunting, culling, keddah in our land, illegal captures and then holding them captive for our entertainment.

However, as awareness grows, so does our capacity for empathy and hope for co-existence. Maybe we will be able to better understand each other in our shared space on planet Earth.

Recent research has revealed that elephants apparently possess names. We can comprehend their communication, which is incredible. What is even more uplifting is that the younger generation appears to be more empathetic than our predecessors, instilling a sense of hope for the future.

Ajay Desai (2002), the Elephant Man of India, made a heartfelt plea: "Saving elephants takes a lot of effort. Some ask why we should save them at all? Apart from all the ecological reasons, I believe we have a moral duty to an animal that has served man for over 4,000 years... A decade with them and it hasn't reduced my fascination and know it is shared by many, including you. There will always be some part of us that will respond to the elephant's varied nature and its ancient association with man... Today we need to wage a war to protect the entire species... To set aside tiny fragments of this vast land; to rein in our greed a little. Is this asking for too much? Especially when this could save both the elephants and us, too?"

The book is aptly titled, "*The Indian Elephant: Endangered in the Land of Lord Ganesha*", and echoes the urgency to act for the species.

"King Romapada's eternal question, 'Now what can we do?' Asked in the context of human-captive elephant interactions posed in *Matangalila*, is still in search of an answer." (Vijayakrishnan, 2017).

When I asked Dr. Sreedhar Vijaykrishnan, a Wildlife Biologist, about his message, he stated, "Asian elephants are one of the most intelligent and highly adaptable species today. In today's anthropocene, amidst constantly changing environments, the array of behavioural adaptations they display is remarkable. From modifying their behaviour to avoid people (in the wild) to picking up and understanding dozens of commands and gestures (in captivity), elephants continue to amaze us through their advanced cognition and learning. Despite years of scientific inquiry, our understanding of elephant behaviour and ecology remains limited, both in the wild and in captivity. And understanding these in both these settings could prove invaluable in their conservation and welfare. One of the things that fascinates me about elephants after spending close to two decades following them in the wild is that there is something new that I observe and learn every single time I am with them. After all these years of studying them, elephants can truly make you feel humbled by the fact that the picture is still not complete, and it, perhaps, never will be. And that, to me, is precisely what keeps me going. This makes it even more crucial to invest more time and effort, and garner more attention and support to understand and contribute towards improving their lives, both in the wild and in captivity, in the days to come." Dr. Sreedhar specialises in Asian elephant behaviour and ecology, working in various landscapes across India and Sri Lanka.

"My mission and my passion are to give people hope."
– Dr. Jane Goodall

There is indeed hope when I witness the dedication of passionate advocates, conservationists and the collaboration of young individuals who bring innovative solutions to protect the species and communities that co-exist.

A notable initiative that has brought joy to me is the work of A Rocha India, which employs trained dog squads to detect elephants. This initiative serves as a catalyst to support the Forest Department's efforts, aiming to mitigate human-elephant conflict in Bannerghatta, an area on the outskirts of the fast-growing Bengaluru population.

In the welfare space, it is most heartening to witness sanctuaries such as Elephant Care Facility and Wildlife SOS that provide a semi-wild environment where abused and traumatised elephants can find a second home.

Cosmic Sacrality

"If one honours God, the sun or the fire, then one honours one's own vital force, the libido."

– **Carl Jung**

Perhaps the Elephants are much more evolved than our human race, patiently waiting to help us reconnect to the world's soul. In this chapter, my endeavour has been to establish a connection between Anima Mundi and Elephants.

By opening our hearts and souls to nature and all its beings, it is possible to repair the damage done in the name of growth. This would enable us to expand our consciousness to the vast cosmos, akin to the concept of Ganesha, an integration of human and animal symbols that has the ability to hold the evolution of consciousness.

We can enter 'mystical participation' with nature by *'soul-tending'* (Smith, 2007). This reverential attitude forms the foundation of ancient rituals that still exist in India and should be revived, much like the Elephant Festival.

A chance encounter showed that there still are people who are deeply intertwined with the fabric of life. As Eliade says, *"All nature is capable of revealing itself as cosmic sacrality (1987)."*

Sidda, a partially blind gentle elephant, enters the space as an apt example to portray the elephant's landscape and co-existence. 'Save Sidda campaign' displayed the empathic connection of people who supported the wild elephant nursing a leg injury from falling into a ditch near Ramanagara, 40 km from Bengaluru. His spirited fight for three months had one and all praying. After Sidda passed away, the dear soul was buried inside the Magadi forest, and the distraught villagers wanted to build a memorial. Let's carry Sidda's message and hold this reverential attitude for the entire species who's lived with us for eons.

The Dream really knows the Dreamer

"What is the metaphoric field within which we are located, and what is the presence, the new experience of insight that is requesting voice."

—Jeffrey Miller

I feel a deep connection with Leela as if she is attuned to me and truly opened me. It's as if the elephant spirit is smiling as I express this. Leela makes her way to my dream world at the right time as we draw towards the completion of the book. Perhaps her way of inviting you to join us in the world of elephants!

It is Leela's first and holding dream as I had hurt myself again, the dream helped to come into my essence and become embodied. Even from a distance, she has held me close, our hearts beating in synchrony.

"I am energetically cleansing Leela in a pristine, high-energy place. She feels relaxed and settles down, beaming with peace and strength."

It's exactly the message I needed, and saw it mirrored through her. The dream was dreaming me, or perhaps the elephants were!

The unifying field with Leela represents the current zeitgeist of our times. It encourages us to move past the separatist mindset that exploits nature and treats other beings as inferior. Our society could approach and connect with the '*Other*' through the eyes of curiosity rather than fear, so that we may take action to protect nature and stop demonising the wild. This connection with the sentient beings is a step towards healing and reconnecting to the ancient bond akin to my vision.

Wings to Freedom

A Senior Jungian trainer shared an interesting dream when she heard the title of the book 'Elephant Wings to Freedom'. The dream goes like this: "Before an important exam/interview, I dreamt of flying elephants and found it holding and reassuring."

Truly, elephants have wings—this is a message from the collective psyche of the divine elephants. May we aid their flight and of our own species! Being one with the field akin to my first dream, where I saw an elephant and the young girl flying as one. As though wishing us wings in our journey of life.

In our imagination, let us envision the wings of elephants, symbolising their newfound freedom as they soar through the skies, much like the legend of Palakapya. By doing so, we can contribute to our own personal development and the overall well-being of our planet. This profound realisation struck me suddenly, like a bolt of lightning, right as the book births!

* * *

Reflections

1. What aids your connection to the flow of life?
2. How do you energise yourself?
3. Do you balance being and doingness?
4. Take little steps to instil deeper bonds with Nature and all her beings.
5. Begin listening to the gentler feminine energy.
6. Ponder on balancing the masculine and feminine states in you.

EPILOGUE

"There is no creature among all the beasts of the world, which hath such a great and ample demonstration of the power and wisdom of Almighty God as the elephant."
— **Edward Topsell**

Finally, here we are at the very end. I am thinking, have I conveyed everything that needs to be expressed?

Anyone who has had the pleasure of observing or spending time with the gentle giants is amazed by their intelligence, advanced cognition, learning, ability to adapt, and their complex social structures. They display deep mourning and grief when they lose a loved one and are very protective of their young. They are gleeful at play, and yet, elephants are elephants, and it's best to appreciate them that way.

These beings have opened my world, my life. Yet, it is difficult to fully understand them, a sentiment shared by conservationists. Perhaps therein lies the enigma—instead of attempting to confine them, much like how we often try to confine people and ideas, let us embrace the wonder of these majestic creatures.

But the reality is, while the elephants have successfully adapted to living with us, have we done the same? Despite facing the loss of their natural habitats and, in some cases, their herd, they are navigating shared spaces with humans. However, do we extend the same level of grace to these magnificent creatures?

There are numerous facets to consider, and the magnitude of this shift is too vast to cover every aspect. The humble intention of this book was to present my perspective and what I have learned, hoping to convey the elephants' message and inspire a change in narrative.

As I approached the final stages of writing this book, I had the honour of attending the India Times Environmental Conclave in Bengaluru, supported by the Karnataka Forest Department. Experts,

Epilogue

conservationists, and policymakers deliberated on how we can move beyond restrictive measures and adopt holistic solutions.

It was truly uplifting to hear that we should go beyond a purely barrier-oriented or civil engineering approach when it comes to providing more land for these magnificent giants. We need to ensure that the land provides the right kind of fodder with nutrients that they require. It is crucial to consider all perspectives when it comes to the issue of shared spaces.

At times, capturing elephants becomes unavoidable, as seen in the recent incident in Coorg. The speaker shared that there have been instances of injury caused by gunshots, and many wild elephants that have strayed into plantation and agricultural land have faced such wrath. It's possible that farmers didn't intend to harm them but were firing shots to scare them away. We can never be certain.

As much as we desire their preservation and freedom, we must ask ourselves, what are the solutions? One panel discussion was appropriately titled, "Living with the Wild". Can we, like our ancestors or the hunter-gatherer tribes, treat these elephants with respect and, most importantly, coexist with them in our shared space? Or perhaps, have we encroached too much into their territory?

We need to strive for a holistic understanding of these elephants. One of the top officials urged us to reflect, "Are the elephants on the highway or is the highway on their pathway?" We certainly need more stringent laws for the protection of elephants as a 'Schedule I' animal in our Wildlife Protection Amendment Bills.

The importance of improved coordination for effective mitigation, as well as the significance of tolerance and co-existence, were highlighted. The significance of buffer zones in restoring biodiversity and aiding climate change was also emphasised. When are we going to understand this intricate balance of life?

If this book has stirred something within you, I urge you to become a champion for elephants. Every small act counts.

Through this, we can begin to question our behaviours, our excessive greed and desires, and our overconsumption. Do we pause to consider what elephants truly need?

Epilogue

It is time for a shift from dominance to connection, embracing the interconnectedness of all living beings. This theme is echoed throughout the pages of this book as well. I discovered a beautiful word encapsulating the book's essence: 'Earth body'—we are all bodies influencing each other, regulating (ourselves) and co-regulating in this shared field—Anima Mundi indeed!

> *"In the racial memory of elephants, long before the dawn of human consciousness, perhaps they, like us, much later, recognised and revered a Buddha or a Krishna in their midst.*
> *Appearing once in every millennium in their own image to guide, inspire, awakening them to the nature of divinity,*
> *the divinity in their nature and the power of loving kindness.*
> *If this is true for us, then the truth we share to celebrate the sacred presence that illumines our mortal lives.*
> *Perhaps elephants are more enlightened Buddha natured, Krishna conscious than we,*
> *a younger species beginning to evolve, recognise and revere to save them from extinction,*
> *giving loving kindness to them all and every creature, great and small."*
> — **Sacred Elephants.**

In this beautiful poem by Michael Fox, my sentiments are echoed, and I sincerely hope that we can forever hold these beings with a reverential attitude.

Epilogue

Don't Take My Mother Away

"Please don't take my Mama... She is my great, great love.

My cradle, the angel wings, the lullaby of my dreaming heart.

She is my temple—beneath whose pillars,

I first gazed at the caravan of stars,

Who follow the moon across the ink-blue night.

Beneath the shelter of my Mama, I am taller than a king, braver than a warrior.

Raise my trunk in defiance—Who would challenge her love for me?

Since my first breath, she lifted me to my feet,

With that mighty trunk—my first caress, my first faltering footsteps.

You see, she is my sun, my moon, my caravan of stars... And I am hers —

As only the constellations above know and understand,

Who guided this journey of love, which has no beginning

Nor end... Infinite is our universe, the orbit of our hearts, our love.

So please don't take my Mama...

She is my prayer, my breathless joy, the song of my heart.

Forever silenced... Forever silenced... Forever silenced, when she's gone.

Please don't take my Mama—My beloved, my great, great love."

— *Sathya Moodley, South African Wildlife Artist*

ACKNOWLEDGMENTS

*T*he birthing of this book has been an intensely beautiful journey—just like the elephants it honours. At every stage, the right people appeared at the right time, offering their unwavering support and guidance.

First and foremost, to my grandparents for instilling my love for nature. I express my deepest gratitude to my father, whose love for animals continues to inspire me—I know you are smiling from above. To my mother, for ensuring everything ran smoothly so I could dedicate myself fully to writing. My sister, adorable niece, cousins, and extended family for their belief in me. And my cherished animal companions for their unconditional love and presence. Heilo, my feline angel—you opened up my soul! And a special mention to my house staff, Mahesha, who went above and beyond to assist me with household chores, taking care of the dogs, and handling clerical work.

A heartfelt thank you to Manasa K.S. for being my sacred ground and guiding me from the moment the Elephants entered my dreamscape & supporting the book from its inception.

To Sonam Kala, my backbone and my true *woman Friday*—your tireless efforts, from editing to handling every detail, gave this book the wings it needed to soar.

My soul sister Jyoti Eregowda for believing and urging me to put pen to paper. Celebrating more than I do! Prashant Shankaran your wishes, "the world needs you" brought me to action. To Ray Dharma, for believing in me and supporting my journey from the very start.

Anushree Thamanna, for bringing the elephants to my world and your beautiful energy with the sacred architecture images.

Much gratitude to Robert Bosnak for helping me relate deeper with the elephants and encouraging me to share the learnings.

I am deeply grateful to Surendra Verma and Suparna Ganguly for their invaluable guidance as I stepped into the world of elephants.

Acknowledgments

A special appreciation to the talented artists—Dhanush Shetty, Satish Kumar P, Sridhara MG and Sujata Khanna—for graciously sharing their stunning images and artwork.

To Pravin Shanmuganandam, for bringing the book to life with a beautiful cover.

A warm thank you to Maana Patel for penning a wonderful foreword.

To my Jungian trainers, Lauren Cunningham and Lisbet Myers, for their constant encouragement.

To my fellow AANE team members, for co-journeying with me on this profound elephant path.

To Avinash Krishnan, Sreedhar Vijayakrishnan, and Vinod Krishnan—the trio who welcomed me with open arms into the elephant realm, offering their generous support and encouragement.

A special thank you to Ananya Gowda, Anita Pinto, and Prabha Dev for their insightful book reads and thoughtful reflections.

To the Clever Fox Team, especially Agalya for their support in publishing.

I also want to sincerely thank Karnataka Forest Department and all the Centres, Officers, Founders, Managers and Mahouts who have graciously shared their space, learnings and precious elephants. Their contributions made my journey rich.

I extend my gratitude to all the other beings who have supported me in unimaginable ways, including my work colleagues.

And finally, to the dear Elez—who have held me so very gently and worked in unseen ways to bring this book into existence. You have been my greatest teacher, and this book is, in many ways, yours as much as it is mine.

REFERENCE & BIBLIOGRAPHY

Anthony, L. & Spence, G. (2009). *The Elephant Whisperer: Learning About Life, Loyalty and Freedom from a Remarkable Herd of Elephants.* Pan MacMillan, London.

Bedi, A. (2013). *Crossing the Healing Zone: from Illness to Wellness.* MA: Ibis Press, Lake Worth, FL. Newburyport.

Baskaran, N., Varma, S., Sar, C & Sukumar, R. *Current Status of Asian Elephants in India.* Gajah 35 (2011) 47-54.

Byju, H. (2022). *Matriarch- Autobiography of an Elephant.* Neythal Pathipakkam Publisher, Chennai.

Bradshaw, G. (2009). *Elephants on the Edge: What Animals Teach us about Humanity.* Yale University Press, London.

Bosnak, R. (2007). Embodiment: Creative Imagination in Medicine, Art and Travel. Routledge, Taylor & Francis Group, London & New York.

Campbell, J. (1959). *The Hero with a Thousand Faces.* Princeton University Press.

David, A. (2010). *Becoming Animal: An Earthly Cosmology.* New York: Pantheon, 1996.

Desai, A. (1997). *The Indian Elephant: Endangered in the land of Lord Ganesha.* Vigyan Prasar, New Delhi.

Dunlea M. (2019). *BodyDreaming in the Treatment of Developmental Trauma.* Routledge, New York.

Edgerton, F. (1931) *The Elephant-Lore of the Hindus: The Elephant Sports (Matangalila) of Nilakanth.* Reprinted in 1985 by Motilal Banarsidas Publishers, New Delhi.

Eliade, M. *The Sacred and the Profane. The Nature of Religion*. Harcourt Publishing House, New York.

Harding, S. (2009). *Animate Earth: Science, Intuition and Gaia- A New Scientific Theory*. Green Books Ltd, Devon TQ9 6EB.

Jung, C.G. (19 64). Man and his Symbols. Doubleday, New York.

Jung, C.G. (1960). *The Collected Works, Vol 11: Psychology and Religion: East and West*: Second edition, Princeton University Press.

Jung, C.G. (1967). *The Collected Works, Vol 13:* Alchemical Studies, Second edition, Princeton University Press.

Jung, C.G. (1989). *Memories, Dreams, Reflections*. Jaffé A., editor; Winston R., Winston C., translators. Vintage Books; New York, NY, USA.

Jung, C.G. (2009). *The Red Book*: Liber Novus, ed. Sonu Shamdasani. New York & London: W.W. Norton.

Menon, V., Tiwari, S.K., Easa, P.S. & Sukumar, R. (eds) (2005). *Right of Passage: Elephant Corridors in India*. Conservation Reference Series 3, Wildlife Trust of India, New Delhi.

Miller, C.J. (1951). *The Transcendent Function: Jung's Model of Psychological Growth through Dialogue with the Unconscious*. Albany: State University of New York Press.

Porges, S. (2017). The Pocket Guide to the Polyvagal Theory, W. W. Norton & Company, London.

Puyravaud, J & Davidar, P. (2015). *Giant Hearts: Travels in the World of Elephants*. Rupa Publications India Pvt Ltd, New Delhi.

Ravitz, L. (1995). *Ganesha: Lord of Obstacles*. Journal of Sandplay Therapy, Volume VI, Number 2, Spring.

Sabini, M. (2016). *The Earth has a Soul. G.G. Jung on Nature, Technology and Modern Life*. North Atlantic Books, Berkeley, California.

Shand, M (1991). *Travels on My Elephant. An Indian Journey.* Speaking Tiger Publishing Pvt. Ltd, New Delhi.

Sheldrake, R. (1982). *Morphic resonance, memory and psychical research.* Parapsychological Journal of South Africa, 3(2), 70-76.

Shor, B (2023). *Soul of the Wild: The Wisdom of Elephants.* Soul of the Wild Publications, Oregon.

Smith, M. C. (2007). *Jung and Shamanism in Dialogue.* Paulist Press, New York.

Sukumar, R. (2011) The Story of Asia's Elephants. Marg Foundation, Mumbai. Varma Varma, S & Kumar, A. (2010). *Elephants in Sonepur Mela. Observations on Population Status, Trade and Welfare of Captive Elephants Displayed at Sonepur.* CUPA and ANCF, Bangalore.

Vijayakrishnan, S. (2019). *Human-Captive Elephant Relationships in Kerala: Historical Perspectives and Current Scenarios.* Gajah., Vol 50, pp. 29-35.

Williams, H. (1989). *Sacred Elephant.* Jonathan Cape Ltd, 32 Bedford Square, London.

Winnicott, D.W. (1965). *The maturational process and the facilitating environment* (pp.37-55). New York, NY: International Universities Press.

Winnicott, D.W. (1971). *Playing and reality.* New York, NY: Basic Books.

Woodman, M. (1993). *Conscious Femininity: Interviews with Marion Woodman.* Toronto, Inner City Books.

Zimmer, H. (1974). *Myth and Symbols in Indian Art and Civilization.* Princeton University Press, USA.

APPENDIX

Photographs & Illustrations Used in the Book

- Illustrations by Dhanush Shetty - Pages 38, 63, 142
- Photographs by Satish Kumar P - Pages 114, 148
- Photographs by Sreedhar Vijayakrishnan - Pages 83, 108, 154
- Photographs by Sridhara MG - Pages 72, 93, 119, 124, 135
- Photographs by Sujata Khanna - Pages ix, 9, 52
- Painting by Sathya - Page 163
- Photographs by Avinash Krishnan - Pages 132
- Photographs by Dr. Chaitanya Sridhar - Pages 75
- Photographs by Anushree Thammanna - Pages 13, 90, 158
- AI Illustrations by Sonam Kala - Pages v, 2, 20, 33, 49, 56

ABOUT AANE

@AANE.TRUMPETING   **BE, BOND, BELONG**

AANE (All About the Nature of Elephants) was officially launched on World Elephant Day, August 12, 2022, with the objective of championing elephant well-being and conservation by a group of passionate individuals.

Our vision is to create awareness and promote a Nature Movement that fosters harmonious coexistence between humans, elephants, and the natural world.

Our mission is to connect individuals committed to supporting elephant well-being and nature, spreading this commitment across communities and organisations.

Our overall aim is to research and integrate empathetic, indigenous models blended with science and psychology for working with these magnificent creatures.

Leaving a Footprint and a Legacy for Elephants –

- **Outreach** - We conduct interactive workshops and collaborate with communities to promote elephant conservation and human-elephant coexistence.
- **Online Presence** - Through social media, podcasts, and write-ups, we engage global audiences and inspire action for elephant welfare and well-being.
- **Media Engagement** - We amplify our message by sharing programs and success stories through print and digital media for wider reach.
- **Innovative Conservation** - We combine cultural events, psychology, and holistic approaches to strengthen the bond between humans, elephants, and nature.
- **Youth Empowerment** - Our AANE Tribe connects youth through volunteer opportunities, fostering leadership and unity under *'Be, Bond, and Belong'* and *#StandWithAANE*.

A NOTE FROM THE AUTHOR

This book is more than just words on paper—it is a heartfelt offering towards a cause deeply rooted in compassion and responsibility. **100% of the author's royalties from the sale of this book are dedicated to the conservation and well-being of elephants.** Your support directly contributes to protecting these magnificent beings and ensuring their future in the wild and in harmony with nature.

To explore the author's ongoing efforts in Elephant Conservation, Animal Well-being, and Indian Sports, please visit:
https://drchaitanyasridhar.com/

www.ingramcontent.com/pod-product-compliance
Lightning Source LLC
LaVergne TN
LVHW041219080526
838199LV00082B/1299